ENTREPRENEURIAL TRANSITIONS IN F

Organic Model, Governance and Succession

TRANSNATIONAL PRESS LONDON

Books by TPL

Entrepreneurial Transitions in Family Business: Organic Model, Governance and Succession

International Operations, Innovation and Sustainability

A Defining Moment: Transnational Nursing Education

Overeducated and Over Here

Image of Istanbul: Impact of ECOC 2010 on the city image

Women from North Move to South: Turkey's Female Movers from the Former Soviet Union Countries

Turkish Migration Policy

Conflict, Insecurity, and Mobility

Family and Human Capital in Turkish Migration

Little Turkey in Great Britain

Politics and Law in Turkish Migration

Turkish Migration, Identity and Integration

Journals by TPL

Transnational Marketing Journal

Border Crossing

Journal of Gypsy Studies

Migration Letters

Remittances Review

Göç Dergisi

Kurdish Studies

ENTREPRENEURIAL TRANSITIONS IN FAMILY BUSINESS

Organic Model, Governance and Succession

Dr Simon O'LEARY

Chris SWAFFIN-SMITH

Dr Rebecca FAKOUSSA

TRANSNATIONAL PRESS LONDON

2017

Entrepreneurial Transitions in Family Business: Organic Model, Governance and Succession

By Dr Simon O'Leary, Chris Swaffin-Smith, Dr Rebecca Fakoussa

First Published in 2017 by TRANSNATIONAL PRESS LONDON in the United Kingdom, 12 Ridgeway Gardens, London, N6 5XR, UK.
www.tplondon.com

Paperback [US Edition]

ISBN: 978-1-910781-66-1

Cover Design: Gizem Çakır

www.tplondon.com

Content

About the Authors

Dr Simon O'Leary is a Principal Lecturer in entrepreneurship and business management in the Faculty of Business & Management at Regent's University London, UK. Simon has published on entrepreneurship and family business in academic journals, books and for international conferences.

E-mail: olearys@regents.ac.uk

Mr Chris Swaffin-Smith is a non-executive Director of, and advisor to, family firms worldwide. Chris runs development programmes for family-business advisors, has taught on family business issues at universities internationally and is part of the visiting academic cohort at Regent's University London.

E-mail: c.swaffinsmith@btinternet.com

Dr Rebecca Fakoussa is a Senior Lecturer in entrepreneurship in the Faculty of Business & Law at the University of Northampton, UK. Rebecca also teaches on family business topics and her doctorate study was focused on issues related to the governance of family businesses.

E-mail: Rebecca.Fakoussa@northampton.ac.uk

Acronyms

ACCA	Association of Chartered Certified Accountants
BIS	Business, Innovation and Skills
CEO	Chief Executive Officer
CIMA	Chartered Institute for Management Accountants
CIPD	Chartered Institute for Professional Development
CPA	Certified Public Accountant
FB	Family Business
GDP	Gross Domestic Product
IFB	Institute for Family Business
IOD	Institute of Directors
k	kilo (thousand)
KPI	Key Performance Indicators
MD	Managing Director
MLE	Medium and Large-size Enterprise
MSME	Micro, Small and Medium Enterprises
OECD	Organisation for Economic Co-operation and Development
ROA	Return on Assets
ROI	Return on Investment
SME	Small and Medium-size Enterprise
tz	transition zone
UK	United Kingdom

Chapter 1
Family business in context

In this chapter, the important status of family business worldwide is highlighted, along with the challenges faced during the development and evolution of a family firm. Links with entrepreneurship, micro, small, medium and large-size companies are emphasised. Finally, the content of ensuing chapters is outlined and extended sources of information are suggested.

Family business is one of the earliest forms of economic organisation and is still the most common form of commercial entity in the world, fulfilling roles across the spectrum of business and organisational activities, ranging from craft specialists, to local mobile food outlets, to online traders, to corner shops, to market sector suppliers, to international brand multinationals. Starting up, developing and maintaining such initiatives requires a dedicated entrepreneurial spirit and a range of management skills, as well as periodic episodes of good timing and targeting. In this book, we have adopted the Miller et al (2007) definition of a family business or firm: "Family Firms are those in which multiple members of the same family are involved as major owners or managers, either contemporaneously or over time."

For many years, particularly since the advent of mechanisation and industrialisation, larger organisations and publicly-listed companies, have been viewed as the foundation or platform for the achievement of economic sustainability, in part perhaps due to the fact that collecting data and amassing information on such groups is relatively more straightforward than doing the same for the many hundreds of thousands of smaller family firms, sole traders and entrepreneurs. However, new technologies are in part simplifying and supporting the introduction of new ventures across the globe, and the economic and societal benefits of family business, and other such forms of entrepreneurship, are being increasingly recognised at official national, regional and global levels. Indeed, family business was identified some years ago by the Organisation for Economic Co-operation and Development (OECD, 1997) as the engine for economic growth and job creation, accounting for two out of three net new jobs created worldwide. In 2017, the United Nations General Assembly adopted a resolution recognising the crucial role that Micro, Small and Medium Enterprises (MSMEs) play in achieving the 2030 Agenda for Sustainable Development, even designating June 27 as "MSMEs Day" (International Council for Small Business, 2017; United Nations, 2017).

Family business challenges

Family businesses and non-family businesses face some unique and common challenges, and it is interesting to take note of the family business challenges listed by the Institute for Family Business (IFB, 2017) as these give an outline or flavour of the particular issues and challenges that family businesses face. Several such issues are illustrated in Figure 1 and include succession, governance, heritage, philanthropy, family council, growth, business issues, sustainability, family office, international issues, innovation, leadership, people, trusts, resilience, wealth, ownership, management and values, with such matters often being drawn together through concepts such as family business planning, culture, vision, strategy and stewardship (Carlock and Ward, 2010).

Entrepreneurs, MSMEs and other non-family businesses face similar sets of challenges, bar those directly linked to family involvement such as trusts, family council or office. However, to varying extents, the business challenges relating to performance and control are common to all organisations. Nevertheless, family businesses face some unique issues and opportunities that are primarily related to achieving the right balance between family and business objectives and aims. The emotional attachments brought about by family-related associations often result in conflicts concerning family and business values, actions and even perspectives in terms of the short, medium and long-term impacts of decisions taken. These conflicts can also become more acute as the generations pass by and the direct influence of the family founder diminishes, and it is therefore not surprising that many family businesses do not survive in family ownership beyond the first or second generation of family succession (Family Business Institute, 2107a).

Figure 1: Some of the challenges that face entrepreneurs, MSMEs and family businesses

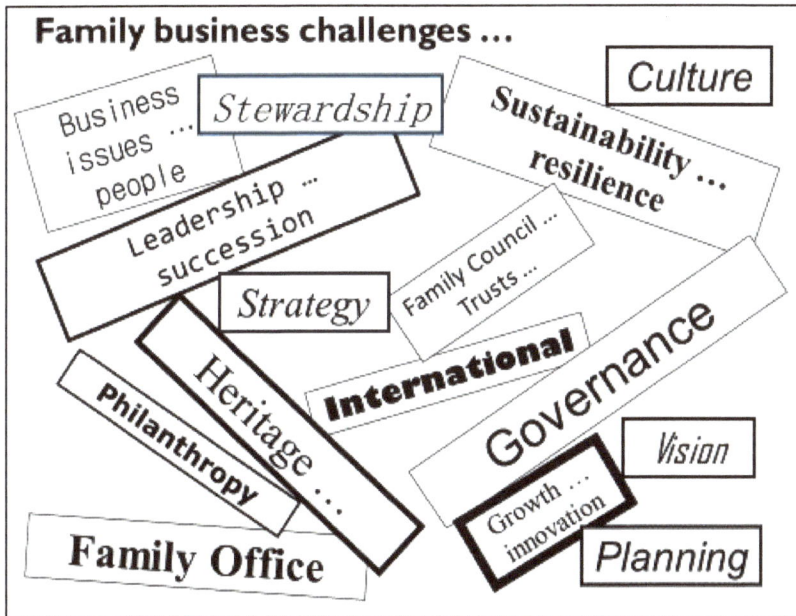

Family business challenges ...
Business issues ... people
Stewardship
Culture
Sustainability resilience ...
Leadership ... succession
Strategy
Family Council ... Trusts ...
International
Governance
Heritage ...
Philanthropy
Vision
Growth ... innovation
Family Office
Planning

Generational evolutions

Having established an initial business, the original owner-manager(s) may, or may not, wish or need to grow the initiative through the combined efforts of a sibling-partnership. Later on, with further expansion, this may develop into a cousin-collaboration and ultimately an even broader family-enterprise. Clearly, such evolution brings with it a series of added complexities, in terms of scale and management, which are likely to require careful attention to ensure success. It is in managing this complexity for the benefit of both the business and the family that adds those extra layers of complication, as well as opportunity, and differentiates a family business from a traditionally managed or non-family business.

Some family businesses are designed and destined to last just one, or part of one, generation, in one location, with one product or service. Some may go on for several generations and then be sold or stopped, while others, again perhaps by design, fate or circumstance, continue for multiple generations and perhaps even transition across market sectors and national borders to create a multinational concern. Each of these phases has its challenges and opportunities, and it is these potential phases and transitions that form the subject matter of this text.

Interactions of business types

Businesses and other commercial organisations exist in several forms around the world, within a variety of regional groupings and across multiple industries and sectors. Descriptions of these businesses vary according to their location, age, absolute magnitude, size relative to others around them, degree of success depending on how that success is measured, function and form. As a result, many labels have been attached to descriptions of these entities, including Small & Medium Enterprise, Sole Trader, Limited Company, Multinational and others. Each of these can mean something slightly different depending on its locations and activities. Therefore, agreed international definitions of these labels, which clearly outline meanings in consistent and absolute terms, do not tend to exist. Some agreed definitions may exist for taxation or similar administrative purposes but this tends to be only on a relatively local basis.

One of the objectives of this book is to bring some clarity to this complexity and it does this by correlating several of the most well-known descriptions of businesses with new descriptions of family firms. Three groupings are used to describe mainstream non-family businesses:

- Sole Trader & Partnership
- Micro, Small & Medium-size Enterprise (MSME) & Entrepreneur
- Small & Medium-size Enterprise (SME) & Limited Company

- Medium & Large-size Enterprise (MLE), Conglomerate & Multinational

The evolution of these four groupings can be intertwined with the development of family businesses (FB), with FB existing in four key states as outlined in the Organic Model of family business (O'Leary and Swaffin-Smith, 2016). The basis of this model, and its relationship with other well-known models of family business, is detailed fully in the quoted authors' journal paper in The Marketing Review and is profiled in this book's third chapter. In summary, the Organic Model outlines the existence of four key states of being for family businesses and highlights the important transition phases between each state.

Those four states are outlined below:

- Personal FB
- Livelihoods FB
- Heritage FB
- Bank FB

The aims and objectives of this book are in part to illustrate how both the evolution of non-family and family businesses are intermingled, and to compare and contrast the challenges and opportunities that exist in each state and transition phase, particularly when the added complexities of families are included.

To help do this, some background to the new business theory 'The Family Business Organic Model' will help. The model was developed by two of the authors of this book and is based on their experiences of both the theories that underpin, and practices of, family businesses internationally. This new business model is used alongside the aforementioned descriptions of the widely accepted evolutionary descriptions of general businesses, from entrepreneur and sole trader, through partnerships, into limited companies and conglomerates. These evolutions are perhaps best illustrated graphically, as shown in Figure 2, and the ensuing chapters, using research and case studies, aim to demonstrate the validity of these descriptions.

Figure 2 illustrates the interactions of a variety of typical business descriptions and highlights how different types of family businesses (FB) fit into that pattern. A business often starts up on a sole trader, entrepreneurial or small partnership basis and this can be equated to the Personal FB. As the business grows it may start to be known as a

5

MSME and a limited company may be formed. In the same way, a family business may also grow and employ more family members to form a Livelihoods FB or a larger company may buy into the business and make it part of their larger portfolio, thus creating a Bank FB if the family still retains an interest. Many businesses remain in this MSME or Livelihoods FB for long periods of time. However, some may continue to develop and form a MLE, conglomerate or multinational, or even revert to Sole Trader status. Similarly, a family business can grow so significantly that it establishes an international brand and presence and so form a Heritage FB. At this stage, the MLE, conglomerate or multinational is often involved periodically in acquisitions and divestments and parts of it are added or subtracted. In a similar way, the family may decide to sell all or part of its business and so form a Bank FB. The purpose of this description is to show how the terms used in family business circles can often be intermingled with the terms used in entrepreneurial circles. One of the aims of this book is to clarify the similarities and distinctions between these two worlds; that of family businesses and that of non-family businesses.

Figure 2: The intertwined evolutionary pathways of both general, or non-family, and family businesses: FB Family Business; MSME Micro, Small & Medium Enterprise; MLE Medium & Large Enterprise

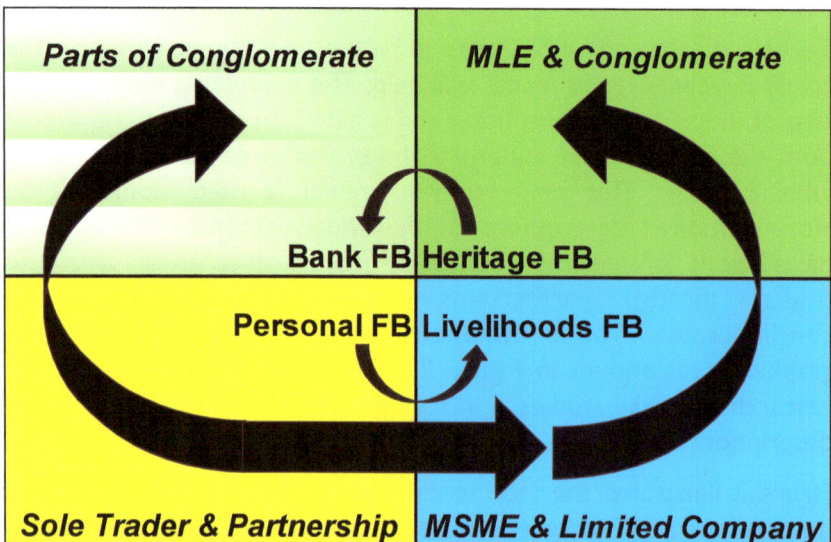

Note: The arrows shown are just some examples of the potential directions of travel across the model.

Family business matters are often addressed in a different way compared to non-family or general business matters and this is understandable given the potential complexities of families and family trees. Family-related matters can include issues around wealth, marriage and divorce for example, while business issues could encompass strategic, commercial or other spheres and, while family businesses often have a long-term and cohesive work-together approach, non-family business can be relatively more short-term profit focused. These though are generalisations, there are nevertheless close correlations between the evolutions of both general, or non-family businesses, and family businesses themselves. This book aims to help enhance the perspective that, although differences do certainly exist between family and general businesses, significant similarities also exist and both of these types of businesses can learn a great deal from each other as well as from studies in their own fields.

The focus of this book is on family businesses and for more detailed information on sole trader, partnership, limited company, MSME, SME, MLE, conglomerate, multinational and other business descriptions and forms, the reader is directed to any of the many other sources available, such as Burns (2016) and De Wit and Meyer (2010).

A consistent colour-coding is used throughout the book to aid the reader:

- Yellow is used for Sole Traders, Entrepreneurs, Partnerships and Personal Family Businesses:

- Blue is for MSME, SME, Limited Company and Livelihoods Family Businesses:

- Green is for MLE, Conglomerate and Heritage Family Businesses:

- Grey or Grey/Green indicates parts of a conglomerate or Bank Family Businesses:

This colour-coding is intended to help highlight how the various issues concerning families and businesses change as the organisation evolves.

The rest of the book

The following chapters expand this initial introduction by outlining some illustrative examples of family businesses in Chapter 2. These examples are then used throughout the book to help highlight key issues and how they relate to real-life family businesses and the challenges that they face. In Chapter 3, the background to the model that describes the evolution of a family firm is expanded upon to highlight the varieties of both challenges and opportunities that exist as a family business develops and evolves through subsequent generations of family members. The final chapters, 4 and 5, focus on four key issues that influence and guide the evolution of a family business, namely the important matters of formality, governance, succession and balancing the family with the business. Finally, together with some final words, a comprehensive set of references is provided as a foundation for further exploration or research on entrepreneurship and family business related topics.

Other guidance on family business issues

While the focus of this family business book is on the Organic Model, governance and succession issues, there are many other matters of importance in family businesses, many of which are covered in far more detail in other books or articles. These other texts often include series of definitions, introductions to theories and descriptions of different types and patterns of family business around the world. Some focus on issues such as decision making, structures or hierarchies in family businesses, issues of personality and style, and variances in approaches to negotiations. Others concentrate on the economics and finances that underpin family business, while cultural and cross-cultural matters are the theme for other authors. For more information of this broader span of important family business issues, it is suggested that the reader make use of the references and suggested bibliography provided at the end of the book. The focus here though remains on highlighting the entrepreneurial transitions that occur in family businesses as seen through the lens of the Organic

Model, with particular attention paid to governance and succession, two matters of prime importance in family businesses worldwide.

Entrepreneurial transitions in Family Business

Chapter 2
Illustrative family businesses.

In this chapter, examples of the Organic Model's four types of family business are illustrated. These are then expanded upon with a sequential appraisal of an evolving family firm.

To illustrate the different types of family businesses described, four examples are outlined in this chapter to represent family firms in each of the four quadrants. Although specific details and names have been disguised, these examples are based on the experiences of the authors and represent the real challenges that family businesses face. Each one is colour-coded so that when aspects of that business are mentioned in subsequent chapters it becomes clear which of the quadrants that firm is in.

As shown in Figure 3, the following colour-coding is used consistently throughout the book.

Whenever examples or anecdotes about family businesses are used, the appropriate colour(s) is or are highlighted to jog the reader's memory about which quadrant(s) is or are under review or discussion.

Figure 3: Colour-coded examples of businesses in each of the four quadrants of the Family Business Organic Model

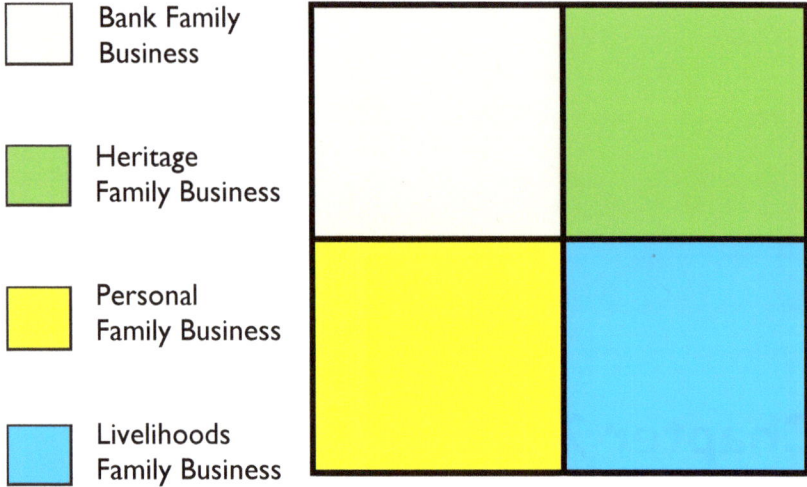

☐ Bank Family Business	
🟩 Heritage Family Business	
🟨 Personal Family Business	
🟦 Livelihoods Family Business	

Source: Adopted from O'Leary and Swaffin-Smith (2016).

CASE STUDY 2.1

'Personal Family Business':

Ashton Gemporium, England

As is often the case, Ashton Gemporium was built upon the interest and hobby of its founder, Jane. She and her husband Paul had three children who were just starting secondary school. For some years, Jane had been making costume jewellery as a hobby and was by now becoming rather good at it. Friends spotted that expertise as well and started to ask her to make pieces for them. Jane accepted and designed and produced in the garage at home, registering as self-employed. As demand increased, she eventually built a more substantive studio in the back of the garage, agreed to also support some other designers in the area by stocking their

products, took on a shop in the local town and started to sell much of the production to tourists as gift products. In addition, she continued to make bespoke pieces for an ever-expanding group of friends, as well as their families and other friends. Her husband was working full-time elsewhere and helped in the shop on a Saturday, but this enterprise was considered Jane's personal family business.

Jane's main aim for the business was that it would supplement the principal family income coming from her husband so that the education of the children could be paid for. There were no formal agreements in place about how the business was funded and so it was, at times, indirectly funded by the husband's income. Jane's husband provided a supporting, advisory and mentoring role. Jane was by nature not a risk-taker and limited the business to the level of risk that she was willing to take to ensure that a balance between business and family life was maintained. She would not borrow money to develop the business, and funding came from the business itself or out of the total family income. Therefore, the business was always kept to a size that could be protected, and the husband's salary was seen as the main family income, with the business income acting as a supplement. Jane's aim was to also maintain a balance with family life such that she would be at home when the children returned from school. At the same time, the business gave Jane a certain status and identity in the town, as well as a feeling of worth and empowerment. The business was successful but there were no plans to grow it and no plans for succession. Once the business had served its purpose and funded the education of the children, much of the equipment was sold, the shop lease expired and the business came to its end, although the expertise was retained and returned to its hobby-level once more.

CASE STUDY 2.2

'Livelihoods Family Business':

Fine Furniture, India

This example illustrates the cultural variety that exists across continents and within the world of family businesses. There is no one-size-fits-all aspect in the field of family firms. There are of course similarities across the world but it is in the variety that exists that enriches the study of family businesses and the challenges that they face on an ongoing and evolving basis.

In this particular case, the family business consists of a consortium of eighteen separate, but interconnected, furniture enterprises in India. With its rich and complex history, India has developed a similarly rich variety of internal cultures within its society and, in this particular example, it is the females of the household who manage the family finances, with wealth being passed down the female side of the family.

Investment funding is provided by family members who have emigrated, often to America or Australia, and wish to invest in the family business. With that investment, the family business is expected to employ other members of the family who may otherwise not have a job and not be able to support themselves or their own family group.

It is not expected that the offspring will take over the business and family income from the business is used to invest in the education of family members. In this way, those offspring can take up a professional career, such as a lawyer, accountant, doctor or politician. If that professional aim is not successful, investment will be provided for that individual to set up another new business and that business will be seen as a one generation activity whose purpose is to help other family members in the broadest sense.

No other forms of external funding are used and the purpose of the investments from family members is to provide employment and development opportunities for other family members. As such, a web of very strong family allegiances can grow in and around the family group.

CASE STUDY 2.3

'Bank Family Business':

Wraps-plus, USA

This family business is different in many aspects. First of all, family funding was used to help kick-start it but the aim was never really to create a family firm. However, it is worth noting that many family businesses did not initially aim to create a family firm; it evolved rather than being planned.

This case concerns two students, Jenny and Lance, who met at university and, near to graduation, decided that corporate life was not for them. They did however also agree that they thought that they could make good progress by working together and pooling their entrepreneurial aims and expertise for a five year period by setting up a series of businesses for selling on and investing in the next idea. Some of their initial funding came from their parents but they were not under huge pressures to return it quickly and this is what reflects the family element in the sense if investment.

Their first idea was a new Wrap product which they started selling at their own university, progressively expanding the business to other educational institutions in the area. Their results were impressive and their business, though still relatively small in the world of catering overall, was exciting and came to the attention of a larger caterer in the area. That caterer wanted to invest in their business to help take it to the next level. To deal effectively with a larger and more established caterer, that meant that the Wraps-plus business needed to become more formal in some ways but needed to achieve that without losing its sparkle of entrepreneurial spirit, the very spirit that had made it attractive to the larger group in the first place. Having said that, the two owners of Wraps-plus did not mind if that was what is needed for them to make enough money to invest in their next big idea.

Jenny and Lance intend to 'bank' their success and are not particularly tied to this industry sector. In the meantime, they are fully invested in making Wraps-plus a success, taking only a basic salary and ensuring themselves that deliveries are made in full and on time. Once the company is sold in full to the larger caterer, they fully intend to walk away and start something else.

CASE STUDY 2.4

'Heritage Family Business':

Wilson Foods, Scotland

The Wilson Foods family business is used later in this book to highlight the evolution of a family business into Heritage status from humble beginnings through Personal and Livelihoods phases. Here the description is a brief overview of its current status. The principal characters are John and Susan Wilson, the founders of the business, their family and close colleagues. John Wilson worked in catering since school and, through the challenges and opportunities offered through redundancy, started up a small catering operation over twenty years ago that grew into the multi-million business that it is today.

Parts of that success were due to personal drive, family support and establishing a good network of clients and colleagues. Over time, more and more family members became more and more actively involved and the business steadily expanded. A significant growth period occurred when John started to meet up with other local business owners, managers and advisers. John learnt new ideas and discovered new avenues for growth. However, this required a substantial commitment to formalising what

had been a set of fairly ad-hoc but successful procedures up to now, in operations, in marketing, in finance and in strategy. John recognised the need to take advice from experts in all of these areas. Successes followed and it became necessary to invest in new factory premises to meet existing, and plan for new, demand. Family members took on substantive management roles with a focus on further investment and growth and a formal Board was formed. Succession plans were developed and the business continued to grow and employ more people. Another new factory was subsequently invested in and the product range was extended. The business overall now held a great deal of expertise across its management structure of family members and close colleagues.

As described in more detail later, the business is heading toward becoming a Family Heritage Business but is currently in that turbulent transition zone between Livelihoods and Heritage. Managing that turbulence is a challenge and requires additional skills and expertise compared to those that were needed to establish the existing business.

The progressive evolution of a family business

Analysis of the evolution of a Heritage Family Business; Wilson Foods.

The purpose of the following more detailed analysis of the Wilson Foods case is to illustrate an example of the lifecycle and evolution of a family business. It is based on a variety of real-life family business cases and, although specific details have been disguised, the aim is not to lose the colourful real-life aspects of the evolution of a family business, its challenges and opportunities.

The principal characters are:

- John Wilson, age 70: Founder of the business.
- Susan Wilson, age 66: Wife of John Wilson.
- Gillian Wilson, age 42: Daughter of John & Susan Wilson.
- Peter Wilson, age 40: Son of John & Susan Wilson.
- Alan Matthews, age 41: Local man.
- Colin Ashworth, age 65: Family business advisor.
- Wendy Turner, age 70: Friend of John & Susan Wilson.

25 years ago

John Wilson had worked in catering since he left school and had been working at the local college in Hertford, to the north of London, for some years now. He and his wife Susan lived close to Hertford with their two teenage children, Gillian 17 and Peter 15. Catering at John's college was being privatised and existing catering employees were being offered redundancy packages. Although John and Susan had not expected this, there was really little option but to accept the offer and think about the future.

Fortunately, John had maintained good links with the staff at the college and also knew the catering people at other colleges locally so, when his own college contacted him to ask if he could deliver some working lunches, he knew enough to confidently say that he could. In fact he wasn't so sure in reality, but could see that this could be a good use for some of that redundancy money and maybe keep the family ticking over for a while. He needed some reasonably priced premises to do the work and found a small empty unit to rent on a local industrial estate. In those first few weeks John and Susan called in a few favours with family and friends, worked 24/7 and managed to meet those first few orders successfully. So, without really intending to, John and Susan had formed their own **Personal Family Business** and were learning all about it as they went along. Over the first few months it became clear that they needed an extra pair of hands on a full-time basis. A local teenager, Alan Matthews, had taken an interest in what they were doing and had also done some part-time packaging for them in those first few weeks. John liked the way he worked and Alan agreed to join them full-time. Over the next few years the business with the college slowly developed and John also picked up a few orders from other local colleges who just called out-of-the-blue, perhaps having heard on the grapevine that John could be relied upon.

John and Susan's daughter, Gillian, started to help out on a regular basis in the front-office on the telephone while their son, Peter, did the odd-job here and there. Over time, a few more local employees were taken on and Wendy Turner, a friend of John and Sally who had worked in accounts with other companies, helped out with the books as and when needed.

20 years ago

John was now a local businessman and started to be invited to various exhibitions and business conferences. He normally didn't go to them but did accept an invitation to one as it was close to home, was on his way to work and they were serving bacon sandwiches. He found some of the talks quite useful and, at one of the breaks, he started having a chat with Colin Ashworth, a local business advisor, who he got on with and who sounded like he had some sensible ideas. Colin also offered, for no charge and no obligation, to visit the firm, take a look around at how the business is running and then discuss further with John. John was happy with this arrangement and agreed for Colin to visit and let him know what he thought.

After the tour, a look at the books and a chat with a few people, Colin and John sat down for a cup of coffee and Colin let John know what his first impressions were, based on his experience of advising similar and larger firms in the area and beyond:

- This was a successful but relatively small family catering business, primarily involving John, his wife Susan, his daughter Gillian, his son Peter periodically, some local employees and a friend to manage the accounts.
- Gillian ran the front-office and one of the local employees, Alan, was effectively the second-in-command of day-to-day operations.
- Annual turnover was of the order of £500k and the existing premises facilities could accommodate a turnover of around £1m but not much more.
- There were no board meetings held at this time.
- The customer base was primarily built upon the father's personal contacts with catering managers based at various colleges in the area.
- The customers normally called to place orders and, apart from that, there was little contact with them.
- At this time, there was only a very limited focus on accreditations across the industry aside from basic health and hygiene regulations.
- Generally, a college would call when they needed a delivery and there were no contractual arrangements.
- The financial aim of the business was simply to balance the books and make some profit, with very limited focus on investment in the business or expenditure such as marketing.

15 years ago

After further discussions between John and Colin, Colin agreed to become the owner's mentor. Subsequently, a series of initiatives were undertaken and other issues began to emerge:

- Peter, the son, married and took up more substantial roles in the business, from delivery, to information technology to distribution overall.
- Gillian, the daughter, started to focus on marketing matters.
- John and Susan bought the existing factory.
- Alan, the local man, had progressed well in the business, ran the factory extremely well and was made Operations Director.
- Colin, the advisor, initiated the start-up of family meetings to discuss the business.

- Subsequently, the son and daughter became Directors and official Board Meetings started to take place with the advisor taking the minutes.
- Two key concerns were raised at the initial meetings: The need for a new factory to accommodate growth and the issue of succession in the future.

The business was now clearly already a **Livelihoods Family Business**. Subsequently, Wendy, the friend who managed the accounts, retired and a financial manager was recruited and a series of financial measures were introduced including cash flow and profit and loss, with investments and depreciation being separated from operational profit. At this point, the Board consisted of the four family members, the Operations Director and the Advisor.

John's wife Susan was by nature more cautious than John about the business and this had helped it become established as a solid £1m business. However, John now felt it was important for him to convince Susan of the need to continue to invest in the business to achieve growth, as it was only through growth that they could firmly establish the business for their children's long-term future.

10 years ago

A major decision was taken to invest in a new factory, using funds from the husband and wife's pension pot.

- The two children were allocated 80% of the shares of the business and the son became Managing Director with the daughter as Sales Director.
- With the new factory, turnover remained stable for one year until the investments in equipment and procedures kicked-in and then sales began their rise to £3m, and eventually £8m by using three additional sub-let factory units.

Part of this success was due to the introduction by the Operations Director of Key Performance Indicators (KPI's) for distribution and operations, using measures such as product labour costings, output, waste and complaints; in fact, there were 20 different distribution costs per product for the 20 different delivery routes used. The KPI concept was to be applied across the business and a Sales Manager was recruited to achieve this. At the same time, salary scales were kept under review and all employees were paid above the market rate and at least at the living wage.

5 years ago to present

Another major decision was made by the Board to invest in yet another new factory that could quadruple the capacity of the business. This was funded in part through the revenue stream and in part by leasing out spare space and equipment in the new facility. The assets of the two children were also used as collateral to secure the loan. A part-time Financial Director was appointed at this stage to help manage the larger financial matters. At this point, the Board meetings became even more formal, were held every six weeks, and produced reports, minutes and actions. In addition, all senior managers took part in an Away-day every three months. A number of key developments took place within the business:

- The product range was extended beyond snacks.
- The business overall now held a great deal of expertise across its management structure.
- The son focused on networking to extend the customer reach, with the aim of securing contracts with major customers.
- The Board agreed which of the various National Awards to compete for.

A variety of business and family issues still need resolving:

- Extending the concept of KPI's into other parts of the business such as in technical areas.
- Considering whether the Sales Manager ought to become the Sales Director.
- A review of branding.
- Rationalising the product range which had grown to 30 while the principal competitors have just 15.
- The company invested in a 40% stake in a small start-up hot-fast-food business that was supplying a university. The two companies are now collaborating on sharing their product ranges and on suitable industry accreditations.
- Other issues include the need to address problems that have arisen from having informal arrangements such as employing a friend as part of the team who subsequently has performance issues that need to be attended to.

At the same time, it is also necessary to clarify the roles and remunerations of the principal shareholders and Directors; the daughter and son have become the majority shareholders and the parents hold a minority of the shares, with the son taking on the role of Managing Director. In addition, it was agreed that the parents would be paid an annual sum for life. Meanwhile, issues of inheritance and ownership of shares in the unfortunate circumstance of a death of the son or daughter need resolving and a family meeting of the extended family will be held to review such matters.

So, the business is heading toward becoming a **Family Heritage Business** but is currently in that turbulent transition zone between Livelihoods and Heritage. Managing that turbulence is a challenge and requires additional skills and expertise to those needed to establish the existing business.

A trio of issues to consider:

- Try to plot the progression of the firm on the Organic Model, identifying key challenges along the way.
- See if you can identify where issues of governance and balancing the family with the business might crop up.
- Explore if any informal arrangements may be better formalised and highlight any areas of particular risk.

Chapter 3
The evolution of a family firm

In this chapter, the issues that influenced the development of the Organic Model are outlined, along with descriptions of other influential models. In addition, the key features of family businesses at each phase of this evolutionary cycle, including its transitional stages, are highlighted using examples and commentary.

Family businesses are critical to the global economy, accounting for around two-thirds of existing business enterprises, responsible for up to three-quarters of jobs in many countries and contributing perhaps four-fifths of global Gross Domestic Product (GDP). Yet only one-third of family businesses survive beyond the second generation, a clear sign that new family businesses are emerging all of the time. In many cases, there is no plan to continue beyond those first generations but in many cases there is such a desire but it does not materialise. Therefore, it appears that the ownership, leadership and management of family businesses requires specialist knowledge and skills to overcome the complexities required for long-term survival. This book is designed to help all of those involved with family businesses better understand the lifecycle and evolution of such entities, whether they last for one generation or one hundred generations. It is hoped that by the end of the book, the reader will have a greater appreciation of the strategic and leadership capabilities required for success in the family firm arena.

This book is based in part on the Organic Model (O'Leary and Swaffin-Smith, 2016) developed to reflect the transitional nature of family firms. That work, widely welcomed since its publication in The Marketing Review Journal, is coupled with further explorations of key issues and includes a rich seam of family business case studies. The aim is to guide you, the reader, through the important stages of the growth and evolution of a family firm by using examples and highlighting several key issues:

- The relevance of governance.
- Balancing the family and the business.
- Incorporating formality and informality.
- Family values and approaches to risk.

Governance addresses such matters as succession, control, inheritance, culture, values, philanthropy, franchising, licensing, shareholders, management and the board. Issues about balancing the family with the business are also included, looking at issues such as boundaries, branding, psychology and gender. Formality and informality is examined, attending to items such as compensation, change, advisors, planning and non-family members. Also included are approaches to risk, differing perceptions of risk and approaches to managing risk. In this way, the aim is to use the Organic Model as a framework to take you through the different potential pathways of evolution of the family firm, signalling key milestones and painting a picture of the direction of travel, as well as offering practical guidance along the way.

The Organic Model of a family firm

The Organic Model depicts the transitional nature of family businesses and reflects the dynamics involved when both business and family issues are intermingled. The model is founded on the notion of finding a balance between the achievement of business and family goals and is extended to allow for the natural lifecycle and evolution of family businesses. The model incorporates a quadrant of four family business types:

- Personal FB

- Livelihoods FB
- Bank FB
- Heritage FB

These overlap and include important transition zones in between. A family business could be located in any of the four quadrants or in one of the overlapping transition zones between them. Larger family firms could straddle several quadrants or have different parts of the family firm in different locations at the same time. A variety of measures can be used to determine the location of the family business, including the importance attached to socioemotional wealth, the use made of professional business advisors and the potential inevitability of change as new generations of family members become involved. This is outlined in more detail in the following sections.

When comparing family and non-family businesses, complexities often arise due to the combined aim in family businesses of maintaining, developing and balancing both the needs of the business itself and those of the family members (Swaffin-Smith et al, 2000). Research has shown that the complexities in a family business can result in a major strategic issue arising nearly every two years (O'Leary and Swaffin-Smith, 2013), in addition to the usual day-to-day operational issues that need to be managed and attended to. Three issues that highlight some of the differences between family and non-family businesses are those of socioemotional wealth, the uses made of professional advisors, and the attention given to new generations of family members. Issues such as these are used to test the suitability of existing family business models and develop the proposed new Organic Model to reflect the transitional nature of family businesses. The research is based on a partnership between an experienced family business advisor and a research academic, an approach encouraged by Reay et al (2013) to help contribute to the communication and development of family business theory and practice.

Figure 4: The Family Business Organic Model, where the four principal quadrants overlap to reveal the important transition zones between them

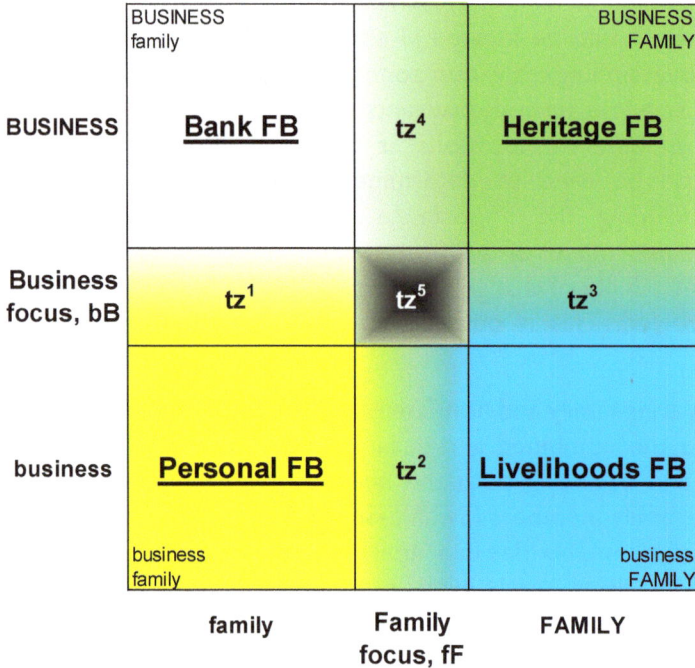

The Family Business Organic Model is based on an evaluation of the aims of the owners, where f or F indicate the focus on family-related issues and b or B reflects the attention to business matters; tz is a transition zone.

Source: Adopted from O'Leary and Swaffin-Smith (2016).

Issues of ownership across Personal, Livelihoods, Heritage and Bank Family Businesses: *The Bank Family Business has clearly transferred its management to others and potentially also much of its ownership and equity to other investors. Contrast that with a Heritage Family Business where it is likely that little equity is with family outsiders. The Personal Family Business is typically fully owned by its founder and the Livelihoods by a group of family members.*

Influences within family firms

Several factors reflect differences between family and non-family businesses and two of those, socioemotional wealth and uses of professional advisors, are suggested as means of evaluating the significance and balance of family values and business focus within the firm. In addition, attention is given to shifts in perspective that can emerge as new generations of family members become more and more involved in the family business.

Socioemotional wealth

The socioemotional wealth of a family business encompasses the non-financial elements that contribute towards the needs of the family and may include, for example, the preservation of the original aims of the founders, the enhancement of family reputation and the recognition of the family for philanthropic purposes (Berrone et al, 2012). Social capital in family businesses has been a cornerstone of much research (Sorenson, 2011) and has tended to show that family firms have a relatively longer-term perspective compared to an often shorter-term and financial perspective in non-family firms, and this can give family businesses a potential advantage in surviving difficult economic periods and subsequently establishing platforms for future growth compared to non-family firms.

Therefore, it is the theme of socioemotional wealth that may distinguish a family business from its non-family equivalent. Nevertheless, non-family businesses do pay increasing attention to issues of corporate and social responsibility and, in both cases, there can be a historical connection between current activities and the founding principles of the firm. After all, many existing corporate organisations started life as a family firm and, through expansions, acquisitions and public sales of company shares, evolved into the corporate entity that exists today. Therefore, a continuation of any founding principles is perhaps not entirely surprising. However, the familial link inherited through family members still involved at a senior level can be expected to have, at one end of the spectrum, a degree of influence at least and, at the other end of the spectrum, a potentially significant impact.

The issue of social capital can be the one binding force that stays relatively consistent as the external and internal environments around the family business inevitably evolve as time goes by. The socioemotional wealth that is inherited and passed along the generations may of course also evolve to reflect broader changes in society and changes in emphasis by leading family members and groups.

Professional advisors

Organisations of all sizes and types often use advisors or consultants to offer specific expertise or new perspectives. The same is true of family firms, many of whom use many different types of advisors and consultants for different aspects of their activities. Typically, these advisors fit into four groups; legal, financial, behavioural and management advisors (Reay et al, 2013). The spectrum of advice can vary from project or task-specific short-term one-off support right through to comprehensive and strategic long-term and multi-dimensional consultancy and support from a Most Trusted Advisor (Strike, 2013). As noted by Barbera and Hasso (2013), the nature, content and implementation of the support will vary depending on whether it is related to a survival or growth phase of the business. It is worth noting that non-family businesses use similar sets of advisors although, with the family elements excluded, the focus may be more on individual employees, groups, teams and departments.

Some family-business advisors specialise in providing advice on primarily externally-related issues such as marketing and sales, while others focus on internal matters such as management skills and teamwork, and some offer support on issues that cover the full spectrum of external trends and internal complexities such as strategy and business development. At the same time, knowledge sharing between the various advisors may be limited for confidentiality or other reasons. However, if the family firm client and the advisors agrees to such collaborations, research by Su and Dou (2013) suggests that such knowledge sharing among individual external advisors enhances the quality of the services provided, the improvements being due to a more accurate identification of the issue at hand, a systematic and shared analysis of the matter, the development of an integrated and holistic solution, and an enhanced credibility being given to the proposed solution because of the coordinated input. Family business research (Kaye, 2005; Poza, 2010; Reay et al, 2013; Sorenson, 2011) suggests that family business advisors can have a positive impact on both firm performance and family dynamics by building trust and resolving conflict. Areas of particular importance include the integration of family members into the business and the issues surrounding leadership succession. The work by Reay et al (2013) also highlights that collaborations between the various family-firm advisors is not a common activity, partly perhaps for reasons of a lack of knowledge of the others' involvement or because of issues of confidentiality, but that such liaisons, if managed effectively, could prove beneficial to all parties concerned.

A successful advisory role if often dependent on forming a good working relationship with the client, one where communication channels are kept open and parties listen carefully to each other's view. The advisory team itself could be made up of more than one person and the client too may well consist of more than one person, so a whole network or web of relationships may evolve over and beyond what may begin as a one-to-one interaction. Certain factors help reinforce the potentially good relationship, such as the embeddedness required to achieve the challenges set (Barbera and Hasso, 2013) and an empathetic and learning approach being adopted by the advisor (Davis et al, 2013). The development and continued maintenance of effective relationships has been an essential element of core texts on family businesses both historically (Colli, 2003) and over recent decades (Gersick et al, 1996; Leach, 2011; Miller and Le Bretton-Miller, 2005; Ward, 1987).

Generational shifts

Helping to develop an individual family member's general capabilities to be effective in the family firm requires relevant knowledge and also the ability to apply that knowledge appropriately. Such skills tend to evolve progressively with experience, not only through education and studies but also through experiences not necessarily directly related to the family firm; for example in sport, in work experience elsewhere, in music, in theatre and other activities, as well as at home. Developing an understanding of when to apply which content and in what context is important in problem-solving and hence important in developing suitable employability traits. In addition, each individual family member needs to become trusted to work both in teams and alone to manage issues and projects as necessary to achieve the best balance of results overall. Studies on employability (O'Leary, 2012 and 2013) conclude in part that content, capability and character are three key factors for developing employability; content based on learning the relevant knowledge, capability being the correct application of that content, and character showing an ability to operate effectively both alone and in teams. This work was based on studies of students and graduates of higher education but the elements appear to be just as important for family members in a family firm. Clearly, the senior and experienced family firm members will have developed many of these traits over the years and may pass on their abilities either formally or informally to more junior family members. In addition, there is also an important potential role for family firm advisors to play in this respect.

It is interesting to note that the current generation of new family firm members form part of what has become known as Generation-Y, a group that is understood (Terjesen et al, 2007) to place great emphasis on personal development and where friendship groups are considered particularly important (O'Reilly, 2000). Such issues may have contributed to Hira's (2007) research indicating that Generation-Y employees appear to be relatively high-maintenance once in the labour force and it would be interesting to research whether this is more or less pronounced in family firms. Family business advisers have for a long time been involved in nurturing and training the next generation entering the family business and this continues today. Nevertheless, research suggests that the current group of Generation Y and Millennials (Howe and Strauss, 2000) who have just entered, or are just entering, the workforce are somewhat different, in part because of growing up during the emergence of several new technologies such as personal computers, internet and smartphones. Martin (2005) indicates that this has affected the way that these people learn and process information, and this clearly has an impact on how they can be best educated and developed.

Business models of family firms

Family businesses have been the subject of much research over recent decades and several models and theories of the family firm have been developed and established. The following outlines the overall structure and premise of a selected well-known "Baker's dozen", or 13, of these and attempts to illustrate what the proposed Organic Model adds to this already rich tapestry. It is quite appropriate that baking is mentioned as a bakery has often been the starting point for family businesses worldwide.

A "Baker's dozen" of existing family business models

In a compendium of tools and techniques to analyse family businesses, Sharma et al (2013) highlight six models that focus on the family business as a whole, and this work complements that with a further seven that address particular elements of a family business. The initial six outlined are the 3-circle model (Davis, 1982); the 3-axes model

(Gersick et al, 1996); the Governance options model (Hoy and Sharma, 2010); the Rules of entry and exit model (Frishkoff and Frishkoff, 2008); the Performance model (Sharma et al, 2013); and the Key events model (Lansberg, 1999). In addition to these, a further seven other family business models and theories exist, including those by Dawson and Mussolino (2014) on Constructs, Gimeno et al's (2010) Complexity model, Reay (2009) on Meta-identity, Litz's (2008) Möbius Strip, Rutherford et al's (2006) Developmental model, Pieper and Klein's (2007) Bulleye model and Sharma's (2004) original Performance model.

The 3-circle model (Davis, 1982) explores the overlaps between the family, owners and employees while the 3-axes model (Gersick et al, 1996) extends the analysis by reviewing changes in each over time. The governance options model (Hoy and Sharma, 2010) attends to the roles of the board and advisors to the family business. The rules of entry and exit model (Frishkoff and Frishkoff, 2008) addresses elements of the transitions between states. The performance model (Sharma et al, 2013) gives a clear outline of the positioning of a family business at a particular moment in time and the key events model (Lansberg, 1999) highlights issues that may catalyse a strategic or operational transition. In Dawson and Mussolino's (2014) work on constructs, behaviour and performance is included along with assessing the socioemotional wealth of the family firm. Gimeno et al's (2010) work addresses the complexities that arise along business and family axes as the family firm develops. A family business and its meta-identity is explored by Reay (2009) while Litz's (2008) Möbius Strip approach highlights the need for a three-dimensional model for family businesses. Rutherford et al's (2006) developmental model extends the models into life cycles, with Pieper and Klein's (2007) Bulleye model showing an interaction between ownership, family, management and business systems. Sharma's (2004) original performance model differentiates between family and business dimensions by addressing the 'hearts' and 'pockets' of a family business.

In different ways, each of these provides a valuable foundation for the Organic Model proposed here, a model where the transition zones are significant. Indeed, it is perhaps in these transitional periods that the key decisions are made to determine the intended direction of the firm.

Proposed Organic Model of family businesses

For the purposes of the model, a family business was considered as one in which members of a family have a significant level of ownership and strategic input, as well as a concern for family relationships. In this proposed model, the relative priority that is given to the achievement of business and family goals is a key factor in differentiating between business types. The research is based in part on a survey of fifty business owners who were asked to identify how they measured the performance of their business, in family and business terms, and to put these in order of priority. Those owners who identified primarily family goals focused on the ability of the business to provide the family with financial security and opportunities for employment, education and involvement in the business. Those owners who identified primarily business goals identified measures such as turnover, profitability and rate of growth. The model reflects the relative importance to the business owners of business and family goals and creates a framework of four primary groups, with transition zones between them.

Purpose of the model: *These typologies are designed to help understand the characteristics of each family business phase and highlight the challenges in transitioning from one phase to another. This helps both the family members and any consultants or advisors to the family.*

Characteristics of family firms in each quadrant and transition zone

The following profiles depict some of the characteristics of a family firm in each of the quadrants and transition zones. Further examples are also given to outline the typical trajectory of a family firm as it evolves and transitions from one state to another.

Personal family firm: In a Personal family firm, there is a relatively lower focus on both family and business goals and, from the owner's perspective, it can be characterised as follows:

- The owner develops a business based on personal skills and talents and does not distinguish between them self and the business.

- The business is not regarded as a family business by the owner, even if family members may help out on a voluntary basis.
- The owner may not have a view on how long the business will survive.
- There is no need to formalise business and family relationships because it is the owner's personal business.

Personal FB's: *There is perhaps no desire to create a mega-business, even if it's a great product or service with huge potential; the founder(s) wish to retain control and therefore boundaries are often important.*

Livelihoods family firm: In a Livelihoods family firm, there is a relatively higher focus on family goals and lower focus on business goals. Here, the owner(s) have a broader view of the firm that can be characterised as follows:

- See their firm as a family business and assess its performance in terms of its ability to satisfy the existing generations' financial, employment and educational needs.
- Tend not to use traditional financial measures to judge the success of their business.
- Do not expect the business to survive the current generation and plan to sell it or stop it once their needs and aspirations have been met.
- Limited formalisation of relationships between the family and business because the family and the business are synonymous.

Entrepreneurship: *As the business grows, employs more family members and evolves into Livelihoods status, maintaining and enhancing entrepreneurship can become ever more important and establish itself in many ways; for example, in supplying for public bodies such as hospitals and universities, there are often supplier framework agreements that must be adhered to. An entrepreneur may succeed by finding a way to manage both of these at the same time, an indication that it is often not just the product itself that is the key to success but the way that relationships are developed. Investing in exceeding quality, health and safety standards may be the key to success rather a focus on the short term.*

Bank family business: In a Bank family firm, there is a relatively lower focus on family goals and a higher focus on business goals. Typically the owners see the business as a means of financing the family:

- Do not view the firm as a family business as it exists mainly because it has the potential to satisfy the family's financial need both now and in the future.
- Focus on the achievement of financial goals, such as profitability and growth, to build a successful business that will help the family accumulate wealth and satisfy personal objectives.
- Expect the business to survive for a relatively long time but plan to sell it as a going-concern during their life time.
- Tend not to recognise the need to formalise relations between family and business as they are seen as separate entities.

Bank FB's: *May be more akin to an entrepreneur who sets up a business, may use family connections but has no real focus on creating a family firm, and has a specific goal such as selling the business. In recent years, many dot.coms have been like this, willing to borrow money and have investors on board. Personal to Bank transitions often reflect a SME being acquired by a limited company. The business may grow very quickly with few procedures in place and, often, formality needs to be imposed later on, especially from interested investors and potential acquirers. The investor may add a Nominated Director to speed up approvals on expenditures, and such support is often welcomed as it helps the founders in their aim of making money through innovation, and perhaps through creating brands, rather than in managing cash flow precisely.*

No realistic prospect of succession: *Sales of family businesses often arise from there being no family successor available to effectively take on the business: 'We've done all we can now for the business. It's worked well for us but our children are following their own careers elsewhere and are not to be honest all that interested in the business, so we want to sell it for as good a price as we can'.*

Bank FB: *The family connection in the Bank segment is that family members may still own some of the business but often have a relatively minor, although sometimes very important, role in its running.*

Heritage family business: In the Heritage family firm, there is a higher focus on both family and business goals. Here it is more typical for the owners to attend to the following:

- Perceive the business as a family business .The business is a means of providing both financial security and an opportunity for future generations to participate in.
- In some cases, it is a means of perpetuating the family name.
- It is recognised that there is a need to measure business performance and efficiency to achieve the long-term sustainability of the business.
- Formalised relations between the family and the business to ensure the longer term survival of the firm.

Heritage FB: Meetings and events often involve younger members of the family as part of their development into the business, such as sitting a ten year old family member at the dinner table next to a senior family member and a family business advisor. In this way, the next generation starts to hear the language of the business and develop a feel for how things work. The Heritage family business may also have several community and social roles, such as for example employing prisoners and offering some of them roles in the business on their release. Many businesses in the luxury brand arena were originally Heritage FB's that were subsequently acquired by a larger entity.

The transition zones

The identification of the four quadrants reflects elements of several of the existing "Baker's dozen" of models described earlier and the proposed Organic Model adds to these by highlighting the importance of the transition zones between the quadrants. Moving from one quadrant to another is not a simple exercise and requires attention to many details. It is during this period of attending to the relevant details that the planned direction may be better understood and subsequently accelerated or reconsidered and changed.

Personal Bank transitions tz[1]: In these transitions, the focus in moving from Personal to Bank may be on growth and expansion, with particular attention given to business effectiveness and efficiency, often taking advice from professional advisors. The transition from

Bank to Personal is more likely to be addressing a retraction in the business and increasing the focus and attention of the owner back on the business.

Personal Livelihoods transitions tz[2]: With transitions from Personal to Livelihoods, the focus is often on employing family members in the business to cope with, or to initiate, business growth. Transitioning back from Livelihoods to Personal often reflects family members moving on to other roles or taking on responsibilities elsewhere, the original owner often taking back full responsibility or passing it on to one family member.

Livelihoods Heritage transitions tz[3]: Having brought family members into the business, the transition from Livelihoods to Heritage is often based on trying to establish a long-term future for the family firm that will continue to involve future generations of the family. The business is effectively being invested in for the future and advice from professional advisors is typically important. A transition from Heritage to Livelihoods may occur if the business is under pressure to retract and recover its strength.

Heritage Bank transitions tz[4]: Having established a Heritage family firm, a transition to Bank status may reflect the sale of the business to a conglomerate whose aim is to extend the brand internationally. The family banks the cash generated and often retain key roles in the business. It could also reflect a reduced involvement of family members in the business and the employment of professionals in each of the key roles of the business, the family retaining a share of the ownership. An immediate transition from Bank status to Heritage is perhaps unlikely as it would probably involve family members, who may have had little involvement for some time, rapidly taking up key roles in the firm.

Heritage Personal and Livelihoods Bank transitions tz[5]: Attempting to transition from Heritage to Personal status and vice versa would involve a complete transformation in the way that the family firm is run. Therefore, it is probably more likely that such a transition would be achieved via the Livelihoods status. A Livelihoods Bank transition may reflect a sale of the business to generate cash whilst retaining some ownership and control in the business.

Discussion and conclusions

Several typical transitions in status can be identified using the Organic Model and Figure 5 illustrates what may be considered some likely candidates:

- **Personal to Livelihoods:** John Smith Limited expanding to John Smith & Sons Limited and later reverting back to John Smith Limited once the sons have moved on.
- **Personal to Bank:** Paul Jones Limited appointing professional managers to extend its international presence, while Paul Jones himself steps back from the day-to-day running of the business.
- **Personal to Livelihoods to Heritage to Bank:** Sandra Wilson Limited employing family members to extend its footprint and establish a strong brand in its market, which then attracts a buyer to acquire a significant share of the family business, the buyer's aim being to build upon the success so far and introduce the brand into new markets, whilst retaining the services of key family members.

In this way, with the transition zones included, the Organic Model complements the "Baker's dozen" of well-established earlier family business models in several ways. It identifies areas of overlap as in the 3-circle model (Davis, 1982), 3-axes model (Gersick et al, 1996) and Bulleye model (Pieper and Klein, 2007). It allows a place for the governance options model (Hoy and Sharma, 2010) to exist. The importance of moving between states is identified as in the rules of entry and exit model (Frishkoff and Frishkoff, 2008). It uses family and business measures as in the performance models (Sharma, 2004; Sharma et al, 2013) and can be linked to the key events model (Lansberg, 1999). It reflects the complexity model (Gimeno et al, 2010) and allows for the co-existence of socioemotional wealth and performance (Dawson and Mussolino, 2014). Meta-identity (Reay, 2009) is allowed for and it fits with Litz's (2008) three-dimensional model for family businesses. Rutherford et al's (2006) developmental model of life cycles is highlighted by the model flow. Therefore, the well-established models and theories of family businesses help form a solid foundation for the proposed new model.

Figure 5: Typical transitions in status of a family business

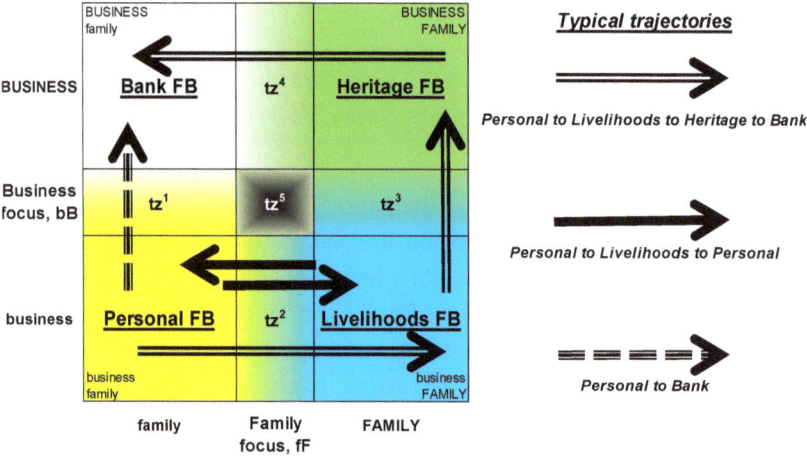

Source: Adopted from O'Leary and Swaffin-Smith (2016).

The Organic Model of the family firm allows for the inclusion of both family and business matters in a quadrant of different states of being, while the transition zones highlight the necessary preparatory time during a change of status. The relevant timespans vary according to the aims of the family and complexities of the business. Socioemotional wealth issues and the involvement of professional advisors within a family firm often give an indication of its aims and direction. Whatever the foundations laid down by former family members, it is also reasonable to assume that some changes, minor or major, are likely to occur because of the organic nature of both the newly involved generations of family members and the continued evolution of the international business environment.

Further research

Other implications of this Organic Model are that, from an advisor's viewpoint, it underlines the need to identify both the family and business goals and how they impact on each other. It also potentially helps pinpoint both the type of advice that the business is likely to need and the advisory styles that are most likely to help the owners move from one type of firm to another. Such transitions may also be related to changes in the relative priorities of family members as they pass through various stages in their own lives. The model also highlights the need to balance these family and business goals if the firm is to sustain itself through the generations. This may be achieved by, for example, continuing to professionalise both the business itself, and the relationship between the family and the business, by developing a family constitution that clarifies the relationship between the family and the business. The authors intend to examine such issues in subsequent articles, along with explorations of the role of an advisor compared to that of a non-executive director in helping the transition of the firm. In addition, further explorations of the model's transition phases may be undertaken to identify the key changes required, the factors that can influence the degree to which the changes occur and the type and nature of support that is appropriate in each case.

Chapter 4
Formality and governance

In this chapter, particular attention is given to the relevance of, and need for, varying degrees of formality and informality in a family business. As the family firm develops, this typically manifests itself in evolving forms of governance and control with the firm. The challenges that such matters provoke are discussed.

During the evolution of a family business, many transformations occur as the business develops and as the family changes. Some of the key issues that arise include the differing degrees of formality and informality that may exist, or may be required, to succeed in the particular environments or sectors within which the business operates. At the same time, perceptions of risk within the family may vary, with some family members being more cautious than others who may consider a certain situation an opportunity to gain ground on their competitors, rather than a risk as such. As both the business and the family develop and evolve, there may also be a need to establish more formal company structures to meet legal requirements both nationally, internationally and also within particular market sectors or operational segments.

In transitional phases in particular, changing from an informal to a formal approach within a family business can also require a shift in culture and values within the family firm and amongst its members. The leader(s) of a business that may have started, or been successfully run, along relatively informal lines for some time might not see a need to change until it becomes clear that there are efficiencies in time and resources to be made. Formality is also important in due diligence processes and if external bodies are showing an interest in that family business. Such entities may, for example, want to invest in the family business in some way, and having formal processes and procedures in place at this time is vital. Informality and formality is often reflected in such activities as human resource procedures for employing and disengaging staff, how salaries are structured, holidays and bonus schemes. It can also be reflected in such areas as reporting lines, sales or marketing processes and the numbers of decision makers. Therefore, formality or informality may not be simply a question of company structure but can also be reflected in the way things are done and, or, seen to be done. Therefore, the values and culture of the business can be just as important, and potentially even more important, than the formal structures that are in place. Nevertheless, the formal structures can provide a scaffold upon which to build and develop effective procedures and relationships.

Therefore, in family businesses especially compared to non-family businesses, personal values have a key role to play in the governance of the firm. In the formative years of a family business, the founding family may govern the firm in a relatively flexible and informal manner to achieve initial successes and respond quickly to events, opportunities and challenges. Indeed, as the firm grows, develops and evolves, it may ultimately find the need to establish a formal Board of Advisors, a Family Office or a Family Council to better manage the complexities involved (Family Business Institute, 2017b). Issues such as these have formed large areas of research and interest in family business studies internationally.

Growth and change

Ward and Aronoff (2011) suggest that, for a family business to continue its legacy, family dynamics must change from sibling-partnerships into cousin-collaborations, with new sets of rules and procedures. They also indicate that cousin-owned businesses are different because cousins grow up in different family environments and therefore often have more varied life experiences than siblings, tend to feel a strong but lesser personal responsibility towards one another, and are more likely to begin employing non-family members in the business. However, the research also highlights that cousins must maintain the strong family bond and establish the right balance between the family and the business. For example, if the business always comes first, then the family suffers, which will ultimately negatively affect the business in the longer term. Conversely, if the family always comes first, then nepotism can lead to business stagnation.

A key transition issue that arises in cousin-run family businesses is in establishing one effective enterprise rather than several different branches. This often requires an agreed set of common goals, visions, and values, where, for example, employment is based on merit and credentials rather than birth right, as outsiders often provide a much-needed difference in view and direction. Family unity can often be lost or over-diluted in a cousins-company and close cousin-collaboration is needed to form a one family approach. Inevitably, such a family is more complex, though it does tend to act more like a non-family or public company.

Personal relationships: *Many examples exist that arise from the short-term informal employment of family friends who effectively, over time, drift further and further into the family business. This often occurs at a time of growth in the family business, when more hands are needed. However, once the urgency has dissipated and the growth phase subsides, it may become more apparent that those same people are actually relatively poor performers in the role to which they were initially allocated or have subsequently moved into. However, as it concerns a friend or friends of a family member or members, this can of course create tension over a long period if it is not effectively managed. Therefore, the benefits of what were initially informal arrangements can, if not addressed or formalised at some point, can often be seen as limitations or disadvantages over the longer term.*

As illustrated in Figure 6, new norms and new organisational systems are needed for smooth transitions from sibling-partnerships to cousin-collaborations. These intergenerational transitions are opportunities to reassess the family business structures and, during this time, cross-generational teamwork is encouraged because the failure or success of a succession is largely based on the relationship between the concerned generations (IFB, 2008). At these transition points, weaknesses can be identified, addressed and hopefully resolved, perhaps with members of the more senior generation becoming advisors to, or coaches for, the upcoming new generation.

Figure 6: Transitional periods between founding, sibling-partnerships and cousin-collaborations in a family business

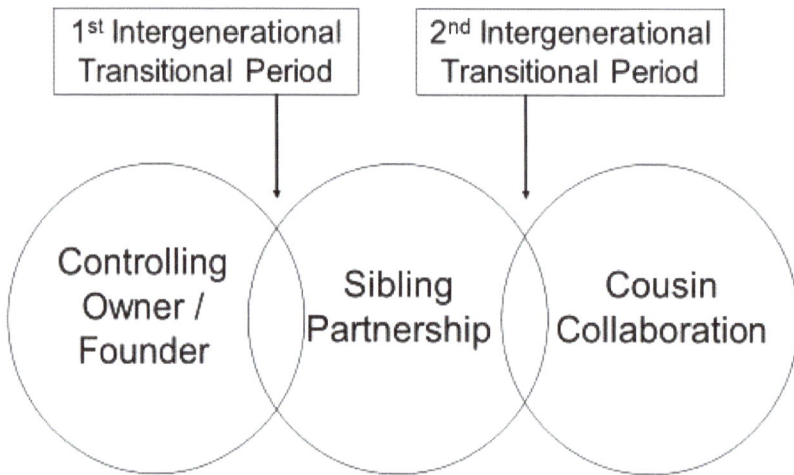

Source: Adapted from the Institute for Family Business (2008)

Patterns of Transition

In the transition of management and ownership towards a cousin-collaboration, the research by the Institute for Family Business (IFB, 2008) indicates that, regardless of the specific differences, each succession stage has a similar pattern for transition as illustrated in Figure 7. This graphic shows the six distinct stages, which can take just a few months or several years depending on the particular family business, that exist between generational shifts.

The first step occurs when pressure builds for the need for change; a natural resistance exists for the change until a trigger sets the transition in motion. The actual transition begins with a period of disengagement that marks an end to a prior era of a former structure, followed by an exploration of alternatives in ownership and management leadership systems. Exploring for new leaders, successors and possibilities opens up choices of opportunities for change. The final stage of the transition is a commitment to new structures, policies, routines, and systems of governance; ultimately deciding to operate differently for the successful continuation of the family business through the next generation.

Figure 7: Patterns in Transition

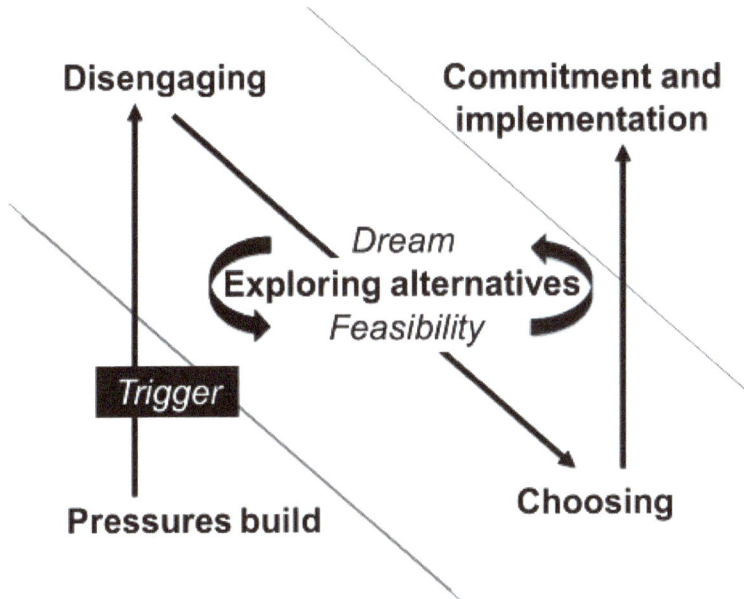

Source: Adapted from the Institute for Family Business (2008)

Figure 8: Ideological phases in a family business

Family Businesses	Entrepreneurialism	Paternalism	Managerialism
Structuring activities	Organic	Clan	Mechanistic
Resource control	Trust relationship	Proprietary ownership	Contractual ties
Business context	Ambiguous	Familiar	Risky space
Time perspective	Emergence	Pat present future	Present future
Success criterion	Cash resources	Ensuring family empire	Quantifiable growth

Source: Adapted from Johannison and Huse (2000).

Compared to a non-family business, a family business carries additional ideological challenges as identified by Johannison and Huse

(2000) and the spectrum of these challenges includes issues of entrepreneurship, management and family involvement, as outlined in Figure 8. At the earliest stages with the founder of the family business, entrepreneurship is often critical while, during the sibling-partnership phase, paternalism often strengthens and finally, during the cousin-collaboration phase, management and structure often becomes the focal point.

Professionalising family firms

Transitioning a family business from an informal management style to a more formal approach is often considered professionalising the firm. Essentially, professionalising the family firm may mean it taking up many of the established approaches that a successful non-family firm follows, with regard to finance, marketing, sales, operations and so on. Onuoha (2012), when assessing family firms in developing countries, identified eight strategies that can be used by family businesses to achieve professionalism, as illustrated in Figure 9.

Figure 9: Strategies for Professionalising Family Firms

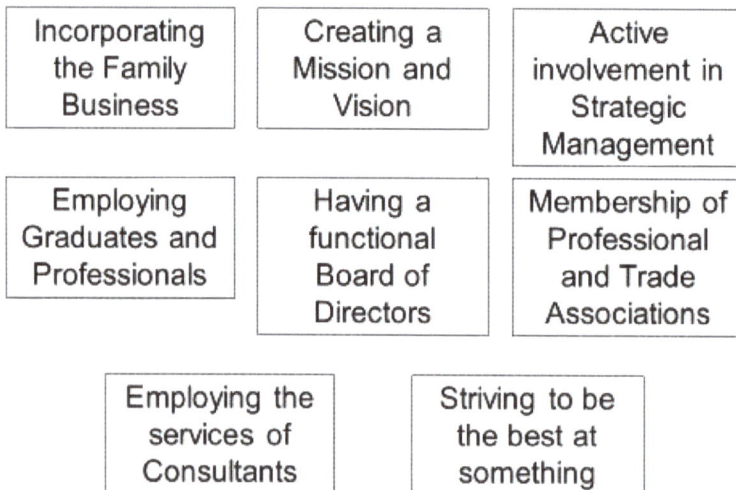

Incorporating the Family Business	Creating a Mission and Vision	Active involvement in Strategic Management
Employing Graduates and Professionals	Having a functional Board of Directors	Membership of Professional and Trade Associations
Employing the services of Consultants	Striving to be the best at something	

Source: Adapted from Onuoha (2012).

1. **Incorporating the family business:** The legal process that gives a business the ability to operate as a separate and single legal entity with limited liability. This allows a company to raise money through loans and creates a degree of security.

The company becomes a legal entity that can sue, be sued and hold property in its name.

2. **Having mission and vision statements:** If a family firm has a mission statement, its reason for existence is explicitly explained to its employees as a basis for motivation, and to its clients it serves as a focal point and brand identity. The vision statement is an internal expression of the company's strategic intent to achieve a desirable future.

3. **Active involvement in strategic management:** The rather short life of family firms in developing nations can often be explained by a culture of relatively poor strategic management. An inability to compete globally is often a result of weak environmental scanning, strategic planning, implementation, evaluation and control. Therefore, to professionalise, the family business needs to institute strategic structural changes.

4. **Employing graduates and professionals:** Developing nations have larger amounts of less-educated and unskilled potential employees. To professionalise, family firms need to reduce nepotism and raise the standard of employment by employing more educated individuals at the entry point. The family firm will then become a more attractive employer to graduates and professionals. Providing regular training and development, as well as appropriate salary levels and other incentives, can result ultimately in higher profits.

5. **Having functional Boards of Directors:** Many family firms in developing nations do not have a Board as such. However, having a formal Board that includes experienced professionals who are not family members, often increases accountability, lowers corruption, improves transparency and thus improves profitability.

6. **Membership of professional and trade associations:** Owner-managers should take part in relevant trade association to enhance networks and receive up-to-date information about government regulations and projects. This also gives opportunities to express concerns to authorities about issues that affect the business.

7. **Employing the services of consultants:** Receiving the services of experts and experienced consultants often provides a family firm with new perspective on the business.

    External expertise can also be especially beneficial in professionalising the family business

8. **Strive to be the best at something:** In order for a family business to continue to professionalise, it needs to make a concentrated effort to be the best at one thing, or in one niche, be that reliability, quality, pricing, service or other. Striving to be the best at something often protects the shareholders' value better and ensures market integrity.

Risk

In everyday life, approaches to risk vary at personal and group levels. Each individual may assess risk in different ways and consider the effect of its outcomes differently as well; some may consider its effect on others just as much, or even more so, as on themselves. This is accentuated even further in a family business and also evolves as the firm evolves. In the early entrepreneurial stages, some risks may be taken to achieve early successes while taking the same sort of risk may be considered inappropriate in a well-established family business because of its potential impact on reputation and the brand. At the same time, the more formal structures of a long-established and professional family business may dampen down on risk-taking to such an extent that reasonable innovations, or even initiatives, may be too difficult to achieve and the business is being slowly stifled or even suffocated. Risks could range from those of a financial or personal nature to those that could damage the brand or relationships within the family and the business.

Risks over time: *Relationship, financial and personal risk can be expected to vary depending on the typology of the family business and its expected direction.*

Governance

There is no universally accepted definition of governance, much less an international approach to governance codes and regulations. For example, the UK has a unitary board system, whereas other European countries, such as the Scandinavian countries and Germany, have a two-tier system with separate management and supervisory boards. In the UK unitary board system, 'insiders' or Executive Directors sit on the Board in companies, and the most common form of voting is single voting. Other voting forms can also be found in European boards, such as double voting and proxy voting, and the fact that these variations exist challenges the assumption made in a number of studies (Gabrielsson and Winlund, 2000; Johannisson and Huse, 2000) that Europe is a homogeneous entity with one system of governance. The regulatory differences between countries led Carlin and Mayer (2003) to suggest that governance structures are not necessarily transferable, particularly when cultures differ and approaches to issues such as innovation and risk also vary. Therefore, evaluations of Board research, especially in the SME or family context, need to take into account national contexts, as differing underlying assumptions and legislative influences exist.

Variations also exist in how corporate governance should be defined; Zingales (1997) defines corporate governance as the 'structures, rights, roles and responsibilities within an organisation', a set of processes, customs, rules and policies that are designed to prevent conflicts of interest. Various stakeholders may be involved in specifying these rules and procedures for corporate decision making, including the Board of Directors, managers, shareholders, creditors, auditors and regulators. Since governance provides both the structure for a business to pursue its aims and a mechanism for monitoring actions, policies and decisions within the company, it needs to align the interests of internal and external stakeholders.

Guidelines from the Institute of Directors (IOD, 2016) outline that effective governance frameworks define roles, responsibilities and an agreed distribution of power amongst shareholders, the board, management and other stakeholders and highlight that, especially in smaller companies, it is important to recognise that the company is not an extension of the personal property of the owner. The OECD (2017) is even more specific and suggests that corporate governance frameworks should ensure that timely and accurate disclosure is made on all material matters regarding the corporation, including the financial situation, performance, ownership, and governance of the company, highlighting that effective corporate governance requires the establishment and creation of:

1. A set of relationships between a company's management, its board, its shareholders and other stakeholders.

2. A structure through which the objectives of the company are set and the means of attaining those objectives and monitoring performance are determined.
3. Proper incentives for the board and management to pursue objectives that are in the interests of the company and its shareholders.

Various professional bodies, including the CIPD (Chartered Institute for Professional Development), ACCA (Association of Chartered Certified Accountants) and CIMA (Chartered Institute for Management Accountants) in the UK, have also set out their own definitions of governance, boards and directors. Therefore, some variety in the interpretations of governance exist, although all of these definitions imply that the 'best interests' of investors and other stakeholders are primarily financial. However, Monks and Minow (2008) argue that these definitions are inherently biased because they have their origins in the separation of ownership and leadership. A primarily financial focus also has its risks as it can promote short-term thinking and does not also embrace the broader societal responsibilities such as the provision of employment and long-term sustainability, issues that can be of particular importance in a family business.

Governance is therefore an issue to consider during the evolution of a family business, particularly when growing and trying to transition from one stage to another. It is in part a reflection of professionalising the firm and it may be necessary to achieve growth objectives.

Roles and responsibilities

Research shows that Directors and Boards play different roles depending on the issue at hand, with Long (2007) arguing that '*There is no blueprint for a directorship that is appropriate for all boards*'. Tricker (2009) outlined that guidelines drawn up with reference to one board may be irrelevant and unhelpful to another given the huge differences that can exist between them. Therefore, differentiation is required and, although regulators have been urged to be more flexible and to take account of smaller, unlisted companies' individual circumstances and context (Mallin and Ow-Jong, 1998), many countries continue to set out universal governance standards for companies.

The European Union (2015) defines SMEs and similar enterprises in its definition: '*The category of micro, small and medium-sized enterprises consists of enterprises which employ fewer than 250 persons and have, either, an annual turnover not exceeding EUR 50 million or an annual balance sheet total not exceeding EUR 43 million'.* However, it is also worth noting the added disclaimer that *'This SME User Guide serves as general guidelines for entrepreneurs and other stakeholders when applying the SME Definition. It does not have any legal force and does not bind the Commission in any way. Commission Recommendation 2003/361/EC, as published in the Official Journal of the European Union L 124, p. 36 of 20 May 2003, is the sole authentic basis for determining the conditions regarding qualification as an SME'.* Clearly, many 'MLEs' exceed these criteria. Corbetta and Salvato (2004) highlight that consideration should be given to the varieties that exist in family businesses as they can range from small, local bakers to multinationals like Associated British Foods (AB Foods), this also reflecting that family businesses exist in each of the four quadrants of the Organic Model. It is also worth noting (Shanker and Astrachan, 1996) that 30% of family firms successfully transition to the second generation, with 12% surviving into the third generation and 3% continuing into the fourth generation and beyond. This is proportionately more than non-family businesses according to the UK Government's Department of Business, Innovation and Skills (BIS 2011). The unique dynamics within a family business could suggest that a different governance structure is needed compared to non-family businesses and that generational issues should perhaps be considered more in Board research.

The Board of Directors is one of several internal governance mechanisms that are meant to ensure that the interests of shareholders and managers are closely aligned, and that ineffective management teams can be disciplined or removed (Kang et al, 2007). The Board, dubbed the *'head of the fish'* (Garratt, 2010) and the *'fountain of power'* (Sundaramurthy and Lewis, 2003), is the apex of the company and its strategic leadership (IOD, 2011). In SMEs especially, there is growing evidence that the Board may be an important company asset (Certo et al, 2001; Gabrielsson, 2007) that can add important strategic dimensions to a small firm (Brunninge et al, 2007; Zahra et al, 2009) and influence value creation (Certo et al, 2001; Huse, 2000).

It should be noted at this point that, while many measures may define value creation in terms of return on investment (ROI), return on assets (ROA) or similar financial measures, this does not need to be how value is understood in a family business, since these firms

53

generally have both financial and non-financial aims (Stafford et al, 1999; Olson et al, 2003). Non-financial measures include autonomy, job satisfaction, balancing work and family responsibilities (Walker and Brown, 2004), provision of employment for family members, being part of the community (Astrachan et al, 2006), and fostering family cohesion while maintaining the family legacy (Carlock and Ward, 2001). Family businesses may also have short and long-term financial goals, from paying wages on time, to providing employment for the family as well as business growth. This balance of financial and more subjective aims and timescales does perhaps highlight a key difference in family businesses and suggests that their Boards may have different types of aims and meetings.

The Board of Directors can be divided into Executive Directors, who are part of the company's management team, and Non-Executive Directors, independent advisors whose role is to protect the longer-term interests of the company and its stakeholders (Higgs, 2002). The roles of the board are '*to define (if necessary), review (annually) and articulate (clearly) the vision, mission and core values of the organisation*' (Barrett, 2003; Garratt, 2010). Research shows that while family businesses are mostly controlled by the family, who may or may not work in the business, the composition of the Board and the number of non-family members involved varies according to the generational stage of the business e.g. whether it is first (founder), second (sibling-partnership) or third generation (cousin-collaboration) family business.

In the UK, the rights and liabilities of Directors and the Board are set out by Parliament (Companies Act, 2006). The Act was developed to define the role of the Director and to differentiate between managing and directing a company (Barrett, 2003). It stipulates a number of duties that must be performed by Directors, assuming that the Board possesses a range of skills and is able to take on a variety of roles. It is these differing duties and roles that may influence the Board, its agenda and meetings, especially in family businesses where multiple duties and roles are played simultaneously. For example, a Managing Director could also have multiple family roles as a son or daughter, husband or wife, and brother or sister, as well as a shareholder and perhaps the Chair. These multiple roles and duties in law, business and the family are what make family business Boards so unique, having to handle additional family-related complexities in addition to the usual business issues, including succession, family roles, business strategy and Board composition.

Family influences

Family businesses differ from non-family businesses in many ways that could include age, size, employee turnover, asset size, industry, location, growth (Jorrisen et al, 2005), strategic aims (Gudmundson et al, 1999), systems (Tagiuri and Davis, 1996) and performance (Poutziouris, 2006). Further complications arise from the lack of a commonly agreed definition of what constitutes a family business; Sharma et al (1996) found 34 different definitions that often varied according to degrees of ownership or management by the family and the potential to transfer the business from one generation to the next. It is often the family involvement and the family's behaviour that makes the firm distinctive (Chrisman et al, 2005). At the same time, Habbershon and Williams (1999) suggest that every family business has a unique set of resources from the interactions that occur within the family as a whole, between individual family members, and between the family and the business, including the unique skills within the business and the brand image which may be termed 'familiness', a reflection of the intellectual capital or resource capital which permeates the company.

Some family members are born into the family business, growing up in and around it. As a result, they are often expected to understand and embody the values of the family business as a form of social responsibility; many being taught from an early age to see themselves as future owners and encouraged to be committed to the long-term continuity of the business. This commitment may go beyond the financial commitment expected of other shareholders and include the acceptance of a 'shared dream' that has moral, behavioural, emotional and family implications (Lansberg, 1999) and such emotional attachment could further encourage family members' commitment to providing medium and long-term strategic direction and a competitive vision for the business. These factors may influence not just the governance structure but the way board meetings are held. Non-economic parental altruism may lead owner-managers to favour family members, sometimes employing their children or giving them their own department within the firm, to the potential detriment of the business (Schulze et al, 2001). Hendry (2002) calls such decisions '*honest incompetence*'; the fact that this can impact on firm governance and how a Board is run makes it even more important to appreciate how family dynamics, father/child or sibling relationships, affect Boards (Hendry and Kiel, 2004). Clearly, family influences can ultimately impact significantly on the firm's position, and direction of travel, in the Organic Model as such influences can have an impact on issues of leadership and management within the firm.

Several differences have been identified between family and non-family businesses in terms of strategy and governance. Donckels and Fröhlich (1991) and Gomez-Mejia et al (1987) suggest that family businesses follow a conservative, less innovative and less growth-oriented strategy compared to non-family firms, while other research suggests that family firms are less export-oriented and less active internationally (Gallo, 1995; Donckels and Fröhlich, 1991). Family businesses sometimes have philanthropic interests, and a long-term interest in their employees and surrounding community, as well as a concern for their own legacy (Steier and Miller, 2010). Westhead (1997) suggests that family firms are significantly less focused on planning-related issues, instead using less formalised management information systems to support decision-making, while Lyman (1991) notes that managers of family businesses use a more personal approach and rely less on formal written policies. This is echoed by Daily and Dollinger (1992), who suggest that family businesses use significantly fewer formal internal control systems, and by Cromie et al (1995), who found that family businesses have less formal appraisal systems than non-family businesses. Handler (1990) suggests that family firms normally have centralised control, and that the rules which govern the family also apply to the business, a view supported by Whisler (1988), who found control processes within family businesses to be characteristically informal.

☐ Personal FB in practice but not in ownership: *Personal family businesses often start on a small basis with both spouses included as Directors even though it is one who is practically running it all. This is usually fine but care needs to be taken in case the couple separate for whatever reason and the business becomes part of the financial negotiations between the two parties.*

Therefore, the unique nature of family business, with its overlapping dynamics of family, business and management (Tagiuri and Davis, 1996), have led researchers to consider the governance problems associated with family control, such as the dangers of bias and the increased likelihood of the abuse of power (Jiang and Peng, 2010). Quantitative research in North America (Smith and Amoako-Adu, 1999) and Southeast Asia (Filatotchev, 2007; Filatotchev et al, 2005) supports the idea that a controlling family can have negative effects on company performance. The results imply that family interests often take priority over the interests of non-family shareholders, with wealth being distributed in favour of dominant family shareholders rather than being used to maximize dividend payments to outside shareholders (Carney and Gedajlovic, 2002), although it should be noted that this research did not take into account contextual factors such as size and turnover. Board diversity in family firms is also important, including non-family Directors and non-family Non-Executive Directors, and it may be that their independent and experienced input may help catalyse a family's desire to transition across the Organic Model of development.

The objectives of family businesses

The overlap between business, family and management can often affect the goals of a family business. Singer and Donoho (1992) suggest that family and business aims are often diametrically opposed, such as in instant shareholder value versus value creation or in best person for the job versus nepotism, although Jaskiewicz and Klein (2007) found that the goals of owners and management are more likely to be aligned in family businesses with smaller Boards. Other researchers have shown how families, and consequently their business goals and objectives, change as they move through the various stages in the family life cycle (Danco, 1975; Tagiuri and Davis, 1982; McGivern, 1989). Sharma et al (1997) suggest that the life cycle may also affect outcomes and processes in family firms. Tagiuri and Davis (1992) conducted an empirical study of US family businesses and found that the six most important goals, from a list of 74, were to:

- Have a company where employees can be happy, productive and proud;
- Provide financial security and benefits for the owner;
- Develop new, quality products;
- Foster personal growth, social advancement and autonomy;
- Promote good corporate citizenship; and to
- Provide job security.

This suggests that family businesses do not exist solely to produce the maximum return for shareholders and it may indeed be more important to the family business Board to retain staff, even at the cost of reducing the dividend, to preserve the legacy of the family. Literature suggests that as companies increase in size, the structure of the Board becomes more complex and firmly set. A number of authors recommend that where a large number of family members have an interest in the company, they should appoint a Family Council or choose representatives to sit on the Board.

The Board of a Family Business

Decision making may be defined as the formulation, implementation and evaluation/monitoring of decisions (Judge, 1989). Fama and Jensen (1983) identified four steps in the decision-making process:

Figure 10: Decision making table

Stage/Label	Description	Application to FB Board
1. Initiation	Proposals for resource utilization and structuring	Suggestions put on/dropped from agenda
2. Ratification	Choosing of initiatives to be implemented	Directorial input: making an argument, leading the discussion, gauging nuances, ending in a voting process
3. Implementation	Execution of ratified decisions	Process and procedures carried out by management
4. Monitoring	Measurement of the performance of decision agents and implementation of rewards	Board evaluates results

Source: Adapted from Fama and Jensen (1983).

However, this work does not take into account the human element, such as the effects of individual personalities and their interaction, and the smooth functioning of the decision-making process often depends on directors' relationships and negotiating skills. Nor are these relationships static and, like families, organisations move through a lifecycle. The various needs of Boards, families and management, and the relationships between them, have to be managed at each stage of this lifecycle.

Growth issues: *Over time, the management structures is some family businesses become so complex that the Board may have up to twenty Directors, with still no agreement on either how long someone can remain a Director and what their particular role as a Director is. As a result, innovation is often stifled and the business cannot adapt quickly enough to changing circumstances. It has become neither effective nor efficient. It is 'stuck in the middle' in a muddle.*

Roles of family and non-family members: *Degrees of formality and trust change as the family business evolves, particularly as the firm grows and the number and roles of family members and non-family employees involved increases. Comparisons, in terms of effort, salary, expectations and so on, between family and non-family members can be particularly important when they are doing similar roles.*

Forbes and Milliken (1999) identified the socio-psychological factors that influence decision making, specifically effort norms (the efforts of individual directors to prepare and participate), cognitive conflict (lack of openness to debate and the exchange of ideas) and the presence and use of knowledge and skill (individual directors' knowledge about the company and the industry sector, and the board's collective ability to exploit this knowledge). Intragroup decision making is further affected by the group's underlying norms, roles and relations and by its common goals. Wageman (1995) describes the interdependence of group members, suggesting that the group collectively influences the behaviours, attitudes, opinions and experiences of individual members. Where Directors share a background or family connection, this interdependence is likely to be even stronger. The emergence of sub-groups within a board, such as a family group, can adversely impact both the decision-making process and group cohesion (Dion, 2000). Forbes and Milliken (1999) define cohesion as the Board's capacity to continue working together despite disagreements. Searle (2010) alerts us to the difficulty of distinguishing whether behaviour '*is prompted by an external event or an internal trait*'. Coulson-Thomas (2007) identified that conduct rather than structure appears to be the key to Directorial performance. Aylward (2005) and Gleason (2004) reported that certain entrepreneurs believed their Boards had been helpful in the earlier stages of business development. Knell (2006) considers the value-added by a Board to be an important aspect of corporate governance, while Charan (1998 and 2005) expresses the view that corporate governance should involve more than compliance and embrace a Board's contribution to a company's competitive advantage. A desire for independence and 'being in control', which appear to be among the main reasons why many people start or join an entrepreneurial business, may partly explain their reluctance to be 'controlled' by a board (Merson, 2004).

Board meetings

Although the importance of understanding Board behaviour is increasingly appreciated, relatively little is known about Board meetings (Carter and Lorsch, 2003; Charan, 2005; He and Huang, 2011). Board meetings are the main collegial space for directors to execute their roles, duties and responsibilities and to contribute to decision making. Current research on Board meetings portrays them as homogeneous and monolithic (Monks and Minow, 2008; Tricker, 2009) although this raises the issue of whether many important decisions are actually made outside the Board room.

The literature offers various recommendations on how often Board meetings should be held and what form they should take, with Davis (2006) suggesting that Board meetings should be held once each quarter and should last between one and two days; Gersick et al (1996) observe that quarterly meetings keep the Board focused on the big picture rather than on details. Ward (2004) suggests that family businesses need to meet between three and six times a year, while Gregory and Simmeljiker (2002) claim that the European average is about eight meetings per year. It has been argued that having more than six meetings a year can cause a Board to adopt a more managerial role; family business Boards that meet monthly or weekly, as is common in some Latin American countries, risk micro-managing and becoming intrusive in day-to-day operations. Conversely, too few meetings may lead to inadequate communication between Board, management and shareholders, and may also signify a lack of strategic vision. It appears that family business Boards often meet formally at least four times per year generally also hold additional monthly executive committee meetings. These are attended by lead Directors, the Chair, the Chief Executive Officer and senior management or each of their equivalents (Ward, 1992). This ensures that the lines of communication are kept open between Board and management, and Board and shareholders.

Good practice guidelines suggest that Board meeting agendas should be circulated in advance of board meetings (IOD, 2011) although, in extreme circumstances, an extraordinary Board meeting may be called for a specific purpose and take place without an agenda. Agenda items may include recommendations from the senior management team, financial updates and other information. The Board's analysis of this material may lead to the formulation of future strategies. Like minutes, the agenda is often confidential but may be used in a court of law depending on the jurisdiction involved.

Some issues to think about

If you would like to, have a think about the following three questions, jot down some notes and compare your notes with the answers that follow.

Questions

1. What is governance?

2. Why is governance important and how do family and business governance differ?

3. Who sits on a board?

Guidance on potential responses

1. What is governance?

A set of formal rules, processes and mechanisms that govern decisions by the family and the business.

2. Why is governance important and how do family and business governance differ?

Good governance could help the business continue and grow successfully, further establishing its presence in selected market sectors, and preparing a firm foundation for the future. For the family, a Family Council is often elected to represent the different parts and views of the family. The Council hold family meetings to gather the views of the family, use the Family Charter as a guide, and renew sets of values and principles as the family and business grow. The Family Council often elects one or more of its members to represent them in the business. These representatives could also sit on the Board. For the business, there is a Board of Directors elected by the shareholders. The Directors make strategic decisions and inform the shareholders about the state of the business at the Annual Shareholder Meeting.

3. Who sits on a Board?

A Board is made up of the Executive, who work in the business, and Non-Executive or Independent Directors who do not work in the business. The Board can vary in size and each member can offer the benefits of their experiences of business, industry, a particular function, the supply chain, the customer base, and knowledge of specialist skills and so on. Everybody is different and each has something to offer.

Chapter 5
Succession and balancing family with business

In this chapter, the importance of being able to find the right balance between family issues and business issues is emphasised, particularly when it comes to the issue of succession. The appointment of successors, throughout the management team, is a key decision for the family business. The challenges and opportunities that this produces are outlined, along with the potential processes and procedures that may be involved.

Succession

Succession is one of the biggest issues that face any family business and is better thought of as a process rather than a decision, a very important process that ought to involve buy-in from each of the family business stakeholders as it can *make or break* the family business. While succession can be defined as *'the action or process of inheriting a title, office, property ...'* (Oxford English Dictionary, 2014), succession in the family business sense involves two transitions, a transition of leadership and a transition of ownership (Kenyon-Rouvinez and

Ward, 2005). In addition, succession issues in a family business differ from a non-family business due to the intertwinement of ownership and management in family firms leading to a different logic concerning priorities (Haag, 2012).

Succession is the essential test that differentiates a family business from a non-family business and the first succession often constitutes the stage at which the life's work of the founding entrepreneur can either continue or terminate, as passing the family business on to the next generation is just one of the options open to the founder. Other options include a trade sale in the form of a management buy-out or buy-in, the appointment of a professional or caretaker manager, or the liquidation of the enterprise (Burns, 2016). However, the focus here is on the generational change option where succession involves passing over the business, the wealth, the knowledge and the responsibility, as well as the legacy and values, to a family or non-family member for dedicated periods of time. It is often essential that the existing Chief Executive Officer (CEO) or Managing Director (MD) acts as an architect for that transfer of power (Poza, 2010) as, in family businesses, the boundaries of power are often less clear and the relationship between family members, ownership and management is more blurred (Gersick et al, 1996). This means that it is crucial to plan the succession process carefully and thoughtfully to achieve a successful transition and retain key human family and non-family capital. Repeated generational successions are relatively unusual and, while around twenty per cent of all family businesses are run by their first generation, and consequently enjoy the advantage of the entrepreneurial drive of the founder, less than one-third of family firms are successfully transferred to the second generation and only about one in ten are managed by the third generation (Poutziouris and Chittenden, 1996). Such statistics highlight the importance, for planning purposes, of understanding the challenges that family businesses face during a succession. A succession is a critical stage in the evolution of a family business and can significantly influences its position, status and direction in the Organic Model.

Commitment of prospective successors

A successful succession is heavily reliant on the effectiveness of the new leader in leading the family business and that effectiveness is in turn significantly influenced by the motivations of the successor to take up that role. Researchers, Sharma and Irving (2005), analysed commitments and motivations in family businesses and identified four principal reasons that motivate a successor for a career in the family business, classifying four styles of commitment as outlined in Figure 11.

Figure 11: Commitments towards the leadership of family businesses

Affective commitment	Based on a strong belief in the organisational goals, combined with a desire to contribute to those goals and a confidence in one's ability to do so. In essence, the successor *wants to pursue such a career*.
Normative commitment	Based on feelings of obligation. By pursuing a career with the family firm, the successor attempts to foster and maintain good relationships with the senior generation. In short, successors with high levels of normative commitment feel that they *ought to pursue such a career*.
Calculative commitment	Based on perceptions of substantial losses of opportunity, investments and value if a career in the family business is not pursued. Successors with high levels of calculative commitment feel that they *have to pursue such a career*.
Imperative commitment	Based on feelings of self-doubt and uncertainty in the ability to successfully pursue a career outside the family business. Individuals with high levels of imperative commitment feel that they lack alternatives. The underlying mind-set in this case is a *need to pursue such a career*.

Source: Adapted from Sharma and Irving (2005).

A prospective successor may also have a mix of motivations that address parts of each of these four types. Nevertheless, though derived from a different motivational base, each commitment style can result in the continuity of the family business, and the research (Sharma and Irving, 2005) showed that Affective Commitment appeared to have a more positive overall effect on a family business than Imperative Commitment. Therefore, it is important to consider the motivations of the various prospective successors. Compared to non-family businesses, family businesses face a unique situation when considering succession planning. In a family business, ownership, family and management are intertwined and this creates challenges that need to be faced. Succession planning can be complicated, and inadequate planning is one of the principal reasons for less successful successions. This could be due to a multitude of reasons, including a lack of strategy, limited governance, too many potential successors, internal family problems or a lack of professionalism. Therefore, an approach based on the input of multiple generations of family members is often a productive foundation to ensure success in striking the right balance between preserving and protecting the vision and values of the family heritage, while developing and adapting to changes in the business environment.

Succession planning

Succession planning is defined by Rothwell (2010) as a *'Deliberate and systematic effort by an organization to ensure leadership continuity in key positions, retain and develop intellectual and knowledge capital for the future, and encourage individual advancement'*. The complexities of succession include aspects such as defining a vision and strategy for the future company, the division of ownership and the training of future management. The process is often time-consuming and requires a careful evaluation of the most qualified leaders, as well as the support of external advisers such as consultants, lawyers or accountants. Much of the classical literature focuses on a special type of leadership change, which describes the situation where, more often than not, a father passes the company on to his son (Gersick et al, 1996). However, this traditional approach may not apply in today's more complex family business successions, since it limits the possibility of a full assessment of transition options and raises issues of discrimination around gender and age. Given the complicated dynamics that often surround a generational change, it is also important to consider how best to prepare a successor for his or her future role.

Comparing different succession models

Literature provides a variety of different models to help prepare a succession, and/or a successor, and a common factor is that that successor development is described as a process of various stages and not a one-time event. Three such models are highlighted in Figure 12.

These three frameworks help to appraise the family business succession planning process from different angles; in the 6-step process, Chrisman et al (2009) consider the socio-cultural perspectives of a family business while, in the 7-step process, Aronoff and Ward (2011) emphasise the preparations required and, in the 8-

step process, the focus is on the succession process as a whole and builds upon the work of Leach (1994). Each is described in more depth in the following sections.

Figure 12: Three family business succession models

The 6-step process for family business succession	Chrisman et al (2009)
The 7-step process of preparing a successor of leadership	Aronoff and Ward (2011)
The 8-step succession process	Leach (1994) and Burns (2016)

6-step process for family business succession

The study by Chrisman et al (2009) arose from a Certified Public Account (CPA) perspective as a means of guiding a family business through the challenges of succession, particularly the financial aspects. Such plans, especially those linked to legal and fiscal issues, often need to be set in place well in advance of their need, particularly in light of any new legislation or regulation. Such early planning helps alleviate, or even avoid, what can be delicate and highly emotional situations at the time for succession approaches. Thus, a 6-step process for the development of family businesses succession was developed, as illustrated in Figure 13.

1. **Ownership, Governance and Management definition:** The first stage aims to bring the family to an agreement concerning their goals and objectives for the family business. Ownership and governance needs to be in-line with the long-term goals of the business. It is essential that the family agree on one over-arching strategy, since non-agreement and inconsistency are key reasons why many family businesses in the third generation fail (Chrisman et al, 2009).

2. **Succession Task Group organisation:** The second step involves the creation of a Succession Task Group, whose purpose is to assess the potential successors and manage the process of succession. The make-up of the Succession Task Group can vary from family members to external consultants. However, the incumbent CEO needs to be involved in the creation of the group to ensure that his or her values are represented (Chrisman et al, 2009).

Figure 13: The 6-step succession process for family businesses

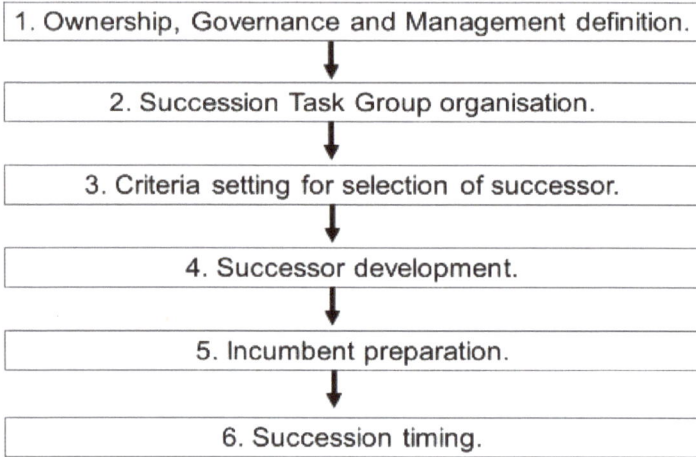

```
┌─────────────────────────────────────────────────────────────┐
│ 1. Ownership, Governance and Management definition.          │
└─────────────────────────────────────────────────────────────┘
                              ↓
┌─────────────────────────────────────────────────────────────┐
│ 2. Succession Task Group organisation.                       │
└─────────────────────────────────────────────────────────────┘
                              ↓
┌─────────────────────────────────────────────────────────────┐
│ 3. Criteria setting for selection of successor.              │
└─────────────────────────────────────────────────────────────┘
                              ↓
┌─────────────────────────────────────────────────────────────┐
│ 4. Successor development.                                     │
└─────────────────────────────────────────────────────────────┘
                              ↓
┌─────────────────────────────────────────────────────────────┐
│ 5. Incumbent preparation.                                    │
└─────────────────────────────────────────────────────────────┘
                              ↓
┌─────────────────────────────────────────────────────────────┐
│ 6. Succession timing.                                        │
└─────────────────────────────────────────────────────────────┘
```

Source: Adapted from Chrisman et al (2009).

3. **Critera setting for selection of successor**: The third step concerns the criteria to be set for the selection of the successor, and these should be derived from the agreed long-term goals and objectives of the family business. Matching the criteria alongside the capabilities of the potential successors assists the decision-making process. This stage often causes disagreements among family members as it may highlight that one potential successor appears to be more suitable than another when such a result may not have been initially expected. However, this is where the agreed family goals can exert their influence.

4. **Succession development**: The fourth step for developing a family business transition regards successor development, and this includes career development and education to adequately prepare the potential successors for leadership (Sharma et al, 2013).

5. **Incumbent preparation**: The fifth stage concerns the preparation of the incumbent leader for the change, an often difficult stage as the incumbent usually remains attached to the family business as a member of the family. As pointed out by Sharma et al (2013), it is critical to clarify the post-succession roles and plans for the incumbent and any

unsuccessful potential successors who will still be involved in the family business, both family and non-family members.

6. **Succession timing**: The final phase of the process concerns succession timing and the importance of finding the right moment for succession. If ownership and management responsibilities are transferred too early, or too late, it can have negative influences on the business. Both the incumbent and the successor need to be ready to let go and take up the opportunity. Moreover, a clear process for transition is essential to avoid confusion among employees and family members.

7-step process of preparing a successor for leadership

Aronoff and Ward (2011) address the preparation of successors for leadership in a seven stage process of successor development, as outlined in Figure 14:

Figure 14: 7-step process of preparing a successor for leadership

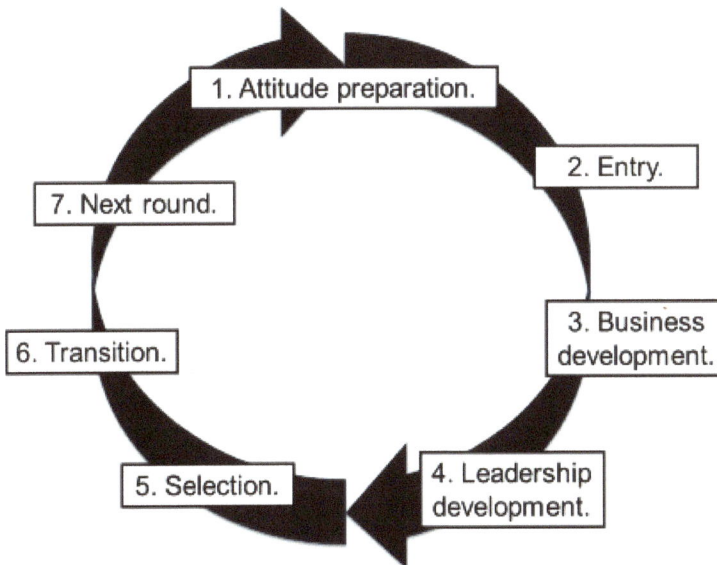

Source: Adapted from Aronoff and Ward (2011).

1. **Attitude preparation** refers to the preparation of a successor for the family business (Aronoff and Ward, 2011). Much of this attitude development often takes place during the first two to three decades of a successor's life and may involve a series of part-time activities in the family business and various excursions with a mentor or the owner of the firm. Ideally this stage also includes several years away from the family business to develop skills and gain other experiences.

2. The **Entry** into the family business describes the point at which the prospective successor takes up a responsible role within the family business and, at this stage, orientation, training and personal development are the key characteristics developing in potential successors.

3. In the **Business development** stage, the successor typically gains significant family business experience and this often occurs when the successor is aged in his or her mid-20's to mid-30's. A range of skills, abilities and know-how are cultivated during this phase but there is no precise definition of the best work experience and it may involve a mix of tasks, challenges and problems. It is also important at this stage to involve the successor in an appreciation and understanding of the company's philosophy, culture and history. This stage may well determine if the successor is a suitable candidate for the leadership of the family business.

4. During **Leadership development**, it is important to ensure that the successor has access to the necessary resources available to help develop the attributes and skills needed for effective leadership, such as understanding teamwork and decision-making competencies. Typically, opportunities to stretch the potential successors will be taken up during this phase.

5. **Selection** refers to the stage at which the final decision about a successor is made, whether that be a determination that the prospective successor is ready and able to take on the role or a selection is made from a pool of potential successors. The decision could be made by the owner, family members, the Board of Directors or a combination of these as agreed beforehand.

6. During **Transition**, the authority of power is transferred to the chosen successor and the successor takes on the ultimate

responsibility for the strategic and operational direction of the family business.

7. The **Next round** refers to a future generational change in leadership. Clearly, this would normally be some time away as the successor has only just been appointed. However, some initial thoughts or principles could at least be discussed at the higher levels in the family and in the family business.

The 8-step succession process

An 8-phase process of preparing a successor for leadership was inspired in part by Leach (1994), as illustrated in Figure 15.

Figure 15: 8-step succession process

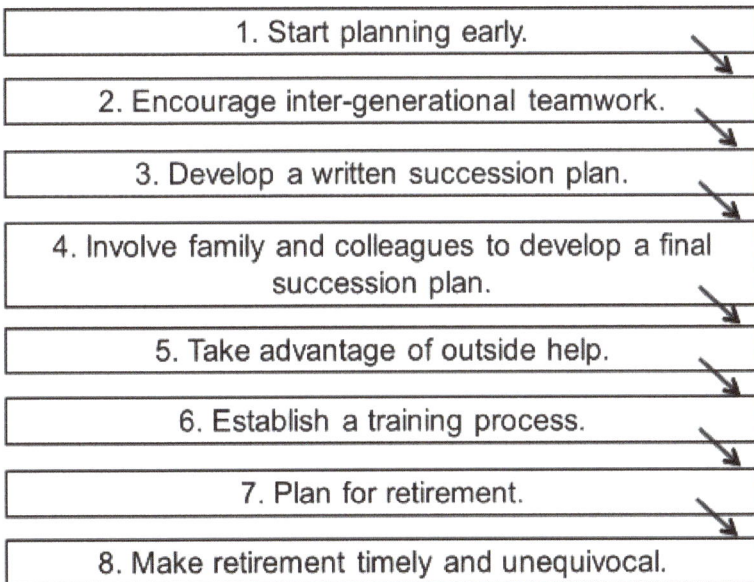

Source: Adaped from Leach (1994) and Burns (2016).

1. The first step is to **start planning early**, which often includes the progressive involvement of prospective successors in the family business so that they start to understand how things work.

2. **Encourage inter-generational teamwork** so that potential successors start to learn from those in the family business and begin to appreciate the types of issues that may need to be addressed by a successor.

3. **Develop a written succession plan** so that it is clear what actions need to be taken to ensure a successful succession. This could require some form of restructuring of the company, as well as an increasing involvement of the successor and a retreat of the predecessor.

4. **Involve family and colleagues to develop a final succession plan.** At this stage, communication is the essential key to success and it is often best to share thoughts and plans with employees in order to gain commitment.

5. It is important also to **take advantage of outside help**, particularly concerning the financial, tax and pension consequences for the founder and the family.

6. The next phase is to **establish a training process** for the successor, so that the best preparations are made for the leadership role. This generally involves training and education, as well as external and internal work experiences.

7. Another important stage is the **plan for retirement** for the current incumbent. This includes both the financial and emotional aspects of having more free time after possibly many years leading the family business.

8. The final stage is to **make retirement timely and unequivocal.** This means executing the succession plan within an agreed timeframe to ensure clarity for all stakeholders.

Each of these models differ in their detail but common to all is that effective communications and agreed plans are important to help ensure an effective succession process.

Former leader involvement

Research by Sonnenfeld and Spence (1989) identified four different retirement styles of former family business leaders. As outlined in Figure 16, four exit-types describe the management styles of the founder or leader of a family business: Monarchs, Generals, Governors and Ambassadors.

These different retirement styles influence both the preparation of the successor and potentially the actions of the successor once in place. For example, the Monarch is unlikely to adequately prepare any prospective successor adequately, the General may become too involved and the Governor may not be available to offer useful advice. Therefore, understanding the likely style of the outgoing leader is an important factor to consider, particularly as the research shows that Governors and Ambassadors tend to have more positive effects overall on the business than Monarchs or Generals. Other research (Sharma et al, 2013) suggests that the best scenario is when the former leader is available for consultation and guidance when approached by the new leader, since the former leader still feels involved and important to the organisation, but it allows the successor to develop.

Figure 16: Leadership styles of former family business leaders

Monarchs	Monarchs are not willing to leave and want to retain close control of operational to strategic issues. May only leave through illness or death.
Generals	Generals identify themselves with the company and plan to be able to return quickly as they assume they will be needed to save the business from failure.
Governors	Governers are willing to leave and focus on other external activities, tend to have the shortest time in office and do not tend to return after retirement.
Ambassadors	Ambassadors lead the enterprise to a certain level and are then happy to leave. They often act as an advisor for the successor.

Source: Adapted from Sonnenfeld and Spence (1989).

The Monarch is the head of a family business and usually stays in the business until forced out. As Poza (2010) noted '*The monarch rightfully operates on the assumption that they will die with their crown on*'. Also, even if they do '*retire*', they can be expected to stay involved in the business, often continuing to take leadership decisions, either openly or by secretive means. The Monarch is often the person who started the family business, has delegated little over the years and wants to keep control of it. This centralisation of power can often lead to animosities within the family business, particularly as it is likely that no succession plans are made and the rules and regulations that govern the business are likely to reinforce the Monarch's role.

The General is the leader who retires from the business with the hopes of returning to reassume the leadership role once again. The General often waits for the successor to appear to make a mistake so that their return is needed. They do not allow space for the successor to learn from even small misjudgements and, while they offer exemplary commitment to the work, their presence can cause internal rivalries as it encourages resistance to the successor.

The Governor is willing to leave and focus on other external activities. Typically, a Governor may not have been in place as the leader for a long period and is therefore perhaps not as tied to the business as the founder or a leader with a more autocratic management style. The Governor is not expecting to return to the business after retirement.

The Ambassador is a leader with a coaching style of leadership, making time and room for the next generation of leaders, and planning the succession carefully. The transfer of power takes place over a period of time and they ensure that the business is in good hands with a capable and suitably qualified leadership successor. The Ambassador keeps the health of the family business in mind and this may mean that a non-family member could take over the leadership for a period, until the next family generation is ready. Ambassadors typically delegate operational responsibilities to the next generation of family or non-family managers but retain representational duties on behalf of the business. They coach, support, nurture and mentor the pool of potential successors. As an Ambassador, their direct involvement in the business reduces progressively, particularly as the successor establishes a position.

Family readiness for succession: Business growth at around the time of succession brings with it its own challenges. The aim may be to pass on the business to a family member but a judgment needs to be made about the interest in, readiness of, and support available for, the successor. This may require the existing and prospective leader to work alongside each other for some time and perhaps for the senior figure to be still at least available for some time after the official handover. It is an issue of the perceived risk to the business.

Succession issues and new family members: *Peter was a management trainee at a long-established footwear family business. Peter married one of the daughters in the family, but subsequently left the business to pursue other opportunities so as to avoid any charges of nepotism. However, when the family business ran into financial difficulties, Peter was persuaded by the family to return and help them to close factories, as the direct blood-family members felt unable to do it because of their closeness to the extended family members affected.*

Balancing the family with the business

When planning the family business future, it is important that both a Family Plan and a Business Plan evolve. The Family Plan is often reflected in the governance structure of the family business in the form of a family counsel, family charter, family meetings or other family structures. It may not be necessary to involve the entire family but there should be clear guidelines for blood and non-blood relatives as well as non-family members about what is required of each party. The Business Plan ought to be clear on leadership succession issues, requires an understanding of the future strategy, the mission and the vision of the business as well as the underlying family values. A successful business plan includes strategic aim for the long and short term, outlining the key performance indicators that can support the business in reaching these long terms aims.

A family business charter is a shared document which gives clarity on issues such as ownership, shares, positions, money, power, performance as well as any possible steps for conflict resolution if this should occur within the family as a result of maybe death, divorce or disagreement. Overall the idea behind a family charter, or sometimes a family constitution, is that there should be honest communication. Initially the idea is to collect family members together and to understand what is important in terms of the family and in terms of the family business. In many cases, a respected non-family member should be part of this process to help prompt honest and open dialogue that otherwise might not occur. It is important to discuss, sometimes over several days, weeks or months, the family charter. It could be that it starts by exploring the expectations of family members of the family business. Other issues may include the ownership and equity structures in the family business and how this may change over time as more generations enter the family business.

It may also include details about compensation plans, or the arrangements for leaving the family business, as well the overall guidelines for governance. The addition of an overview of the family business history could also help highlight the relevance of the values and the beliefs of the family.

When creating a family plan or a business plan, an objective third-view and professional support is desirable, as having the external view of a non-family member as a critical friend could help identify and traverse issues that could possibly arise. When looking at planning for both the family and the business, education and training can be critical. This could be the education of the current and next generation, and may include appreciations of both the challenges and opportunities for the family business.

Effective planning, particularly during the good times for the family business, helps ensure that, when challenges arise, everything has already been discussed in principle and the necessary actions can be taken quickly. Such issues could range from having succession plans in place to necessary changes in strategy. As the family and the business are interlinked, both need to have plans in place:

- Needs both a Family Plan as well as a Business Plan.
- Entire family involvement not necessary.
- Professional support desirable.
- Education and training critical.

Family values

The values and culture within the family are often reflected in the family business. These could be values of honesty, integrity and trust and may be visible, for example, in the way that non-family members are treated. It could be visible in organisational culture and in the values, beliefs and principles of each family business member. These could be reflected in the understandings of the history of the family business, to its product, technologies and strategy, as well as the management styles employed within the family business. In the business, there are likely to be explicitly stated values, policies, beliefs and structures and these ought to reflect the underlying family values and culture as well. This could be demonstrated through shared assumptions and traditions and perhaps through 'unwritten rules' or stories about how people, money, processes are treated in this family business. The visible cultural elements can often be found in its organisational charts, manners, the structures, the products and the mission statements, as well as in the physical environment. For example, perhaps everybody sits and eats together or perhaps elements of strict hierarchy are in place. The paradigm of culture by (Johnson et al, 2011) suggests that there are six paradigms of culture; stories, symbols, power structures, routines and rituals, control systems and organisational structures. Each of these has a role to play in the family business, and may determine how the family interact with its employees with other stake holders.

Family Values: Company values tend to differ depending on the long-term anticipated direction of the firm. If the plan is to sell the business at as high a price as possible, then it is likely that there will be strong focus on costs and revenues. Therefore, suppliers are likely to be kept under pressure and growth of the customer base will be vital. Depending on the aggressiveness of the management approach, staff may also be under pressure and cases of unfair dismissal may arise. On the other hand, if the aim is to create a Livelihoods Family Business, then it is more likely that care will be taken with family members, the focus on efficiency or sickness may be relatively lighter, and in general a supportive atmosphere will prevail. Nevertheless, the business needs to be profitable in the long run to ensure its survival. At the same time, it is also likely that good relationships will be developed with the local community. Family members may be supported but should not be out of their depth as this may cause problems with other stakeholders in the business. So family values are important but need to be balanced against the potential risks involved.

Family vision

The vision of a family business needs to be established through its family values. The family needs to be clear about its vision and its values, particularly if the family business carries the family name and if the aim of the family ownership is multi-generational as reflected, for example, in a desire to achieve, or retain, Heritage FB status in the Organic Model. Each generation is then responsible for the stewardship of the business and doing the best it can to pass it on to the next generation. Therefore, it is critically important that such a family vision of ownership and leadership is communicated clearly and consistently to both the family members and to the business. This could include developing the next generation through successful education both within the company and elsewhere, as well as ensuring that suitable support mechanisms exist if the next leader could be a non-family member whose role is to mentor the next family member coming through. Keys to success include:

- Building commitment through family and business activities.
- Establishing the aim of family ownership of business issues across the generations.
- Ensuring effective leadership development.

Family strategy

Within the family business there needs to be a clear alignment of both financial and human capital. This alignment needs to be in terms of compensation and reinvestment as well as in terms of its people. There might for example be plans that, if the engagement of the family or the family commitment is relatively low, then selling parts or all of the family business might be the best option for the family and the family business as a whole, as reflected in Bank FB status the Organic Model. Declining interest can often lead to declining profits because of disengagement and non-alignment. If the family has for some time seen the business as a source of cash and depleted its resources, there is often little chance to repair the business as they would have to change their strategy and start reinvesting in the business. Alternatively, if the family has continuously reinvested in the family business but needs to extract some cash, this may require a change in strategy. Important issues include:

- Align financial and human capital.
- Sell or harvest areas with low family commitment.

Succession and changes of plans: Sometimes a family business may have been around for several generations, is still doing okay but is no longer the lively developing business that it once was. At the same time, it may have established a substantial asset base in property for example and it is this property that effectively holds the value of the family business. Therefore, that value can be released by selling the business and/or the property. It can happen that the property is actually worth more to the right buyer than the business and examples of this exist particularly when there is a property boom. As a result, many family businesses cease to trade and the value is dispersed amongst the remaining family members.

The Family Board and Family Council

Creating a Board of Directors for a family business can be a daunting task. Founding owners may struggle to let non-family members in but, if the family members have been running the business in their own way for a long time, an independent and external view and expertise can be very beneficial. This external expertise needs to come from a respected and trusted source that shares similar values and understands the vision of both the family and the business. At the same time, that person needs to have the respect, personal strength and understanding to be able to challenge family members in the right way. If a Family Board cannot decide on an issue, then an independent voice can often help break the deadlock and reopen the communications. It is particularly important to have the right governance structures in place at times of leadership or business transition, such as entering into different markets, ending part of the business, harvesting, reinvesting, and selling. At times like these, internal communication is important and a Family Charter, Family Counsel or Family Constitution can help clarify how the family should behave and act. There ought to be a clear case for how transition should be managed and understood and how this should be communicated, not just internally, but also with external stakeholders.

During leadership transitions, shareholder agreements need to be legally binding and reflect national laws. Shareholder agreements, shares and dividend policies should be included in the vision and values that the family and family business hold. Each of these may cover key aspects such as:

- The inclusion of independent views.
- Attention to transition issues.
- Family behaviour agreement.
- Shareholder agreements.

Having proper governance procedures, such as a Board of Directors for the business and a Family Council for the family, can help ensure a fair and strong family business for the future.

Final words

All family businesses are unique, have different dynamics and all decisions that need to be made have to fit within the values and culture of the family group. The aim of this book has been to expose the reader to both the opportunities and challenges that face both entrepreneurs, who may be embarking, knowingly or unknowingly, on the road towards the formation of a family businesses, and established family businesses. It is hoped that the various chapters have, with examples, outlined the common threads that exist between MSMEs, entrepreneurs and family firms. The evolution of such businesses is addressed in part by the Organic Model and highlights the potential transitions between Personal, Livelihoods, Bank and Heritage formats within family businesses. Such evolutionary changes and transitions raise several key challenges and opportunities for success. Of particular note are the requirements for suitable degrees of formality and governance, as well as effective succession planning and achieving the right balance between family and business issues.

Suggested reading

The full list of References follows but the following shortlist of three has been picked out as particularly useful sources of wider information on the issues raised in this book:

- Carlock, R.S and Ward, J.L. (2001), Strategic Planning for The Family Business: Parallel Planning to Unify the Family and Business, Palgrave Macmillan, Basingstoke.
- Gimeno, A., Baulenas, G. and Coma-Gros, J. (2010), Family Business Models: Practical Solutions for the Family Business, Palgrave Macmillan, Basingstoke.
- O'Leary, S. and Swaffin-Smith, C. (2016), Organic model to reflect the transitional nature of family firms, The Marketing Review, Vol.16, No.3, pp.285-297.

These three also include comprehensive suggestions for extended reading.

References

The following list of references is intended to both endorse the opinions expressed in this text and to promote further study of, and research into, the fascinating topic of entrepreneurial transitions in family business.

Aronoff, C., McClure, S. and Ward, J. (2011), Family Business Succession: The Final Test of Greatness, Palgrave Macmillan, New York.

Astrachan J.H. , Keyt A. , Lane S. and McMillan K. (2006), Generic Models for Family Business Boards of Directors, in Poutziouris, P.Z., Smyrnios, K.X. and Klein, S.B. (Eds.), Handbook of Research on Family Business, Edward Elgar, Cheltenham.

Aylward, M. (2005), Entrepreneurship and Governance: A Study on Incompatibility, paper presented to 8th International Conference on Corporate Governance and Board Leadership, Henley, 11–13 October.

Barbera, F. and Hasso, T. (2013), Do We Need to Use an Accountant? The Sales Growth and Survival Benefits to Family SMEs, Family Business Review, Vol.26, No.3, pp.271-292.

Barrett, R. (2003), Vocational Business: Training, Developing and Motivating People. Nelson Thornes, Cheltenham.

Berrone P., Cruz C. and Gomez-Mejia L.R. (2012), Socioemotional Wealth in Family Firms: Theoretical Dimensions, Assessment Approaches, and Agenda for Future Research, Family Business Review, Vol.25, No.3, pp.258-279.

BIS (2011), Business population estimates for the UK and regions 2010, Statistical Release: Department for Business, Innovation and Skills, UK Government, London.

Brunninge, O., Nordqvist, M. and Wiklund, J. (2007), Corporate Governance and Strategic Change in SMEs: The Effects of Ownership, Board Composition and Top Management Teams, Small Business Economics, Vol.29, No.3, pp.295-308.

Burns, P. (2016). Entrepreneurship and Small Business: Start-Up, Growth and Maturity. Palgrave Macmillan, New York.

Carlin, W. and Mayer, C. (2003), Finance, investment, and growth, Journal of Financial Economics, Vol.69, No.1, pp.191-226.

Carlock, R.S and Ward, J.L. (2001), Strategic Planning for The Family Business: Parallel Planning to Unify the Family and Business, Palgrave Macmillan, Basingstoke.

Carlock, R. and Ward, J. (2010), When Family Businesses are Best: The Parallel Planning Process for Family Harmony and Business Success, Palgrave Macmillan, London.

Carney, M. and Gedajlovic, E. (2002), The Coupling of Ownership and Control and the Allocation of Financial Resources: Evidence from Hong Kong, Journal of Management Studies, Vol.39, No.1, pp.123-146.

Carter, C.B. and Lorsch, J. W. (2003), Back to the Drawing Board: Designing Corporate Boards for a Complex World, Harvard Business Press, Massachusetts.

Certo, S.T., Daily, C.M. and Dalton, D.R. (2001), Signalling firm value through board structure: An investigation of initial public offerings, Entrepreneurship Theory & Practice, Vol.26, No.2, pp.33-50.

Charan, R. (1998), Boards at Work: How Corporate Boards Create Competitive Advantage, Jossey Bass, San Francisco.

Charan, R. (2005), Ending the CEO Succession Crisis, Harvard Business Review, February issue.

Chrisman, J.J., Chua, J.H. and Sharma, P. (2005), Trends and directions in the development of strategic management theory of the family firm, Entrepreneurship Theory and Practice, Vol.29, No.5, pp.555-575.

Chrisman, J.J., Chua, J.H. and Kellermanns, F.W. (2009), Priorities, resource stocks, and performance in family and nonfamily firms, Entrepreneurship Theory and Practice, Vol.33, No.3, pp.739-760.

Companies Act (2006), Chapter 46, UK Government, London.

Colli, A. (2003), The History of Family Business 1850-2000, Cambridge University Press, Cambridge.

Corbetta, G. and Salvato, C. (2004), Self-serving or self-actualizing? Models of man and agency costs in different types of family firms: A commentary on "Comparing the agency costs of family and non-family firms: Conceptual issues and exploratory evidence", Entrepreneurship Theory and Practice, Vol.28, No.4, pp.355-362.

Coulson-Thomas, C. (2007), Developing Directors: A handbook for building an effective boardroom team, Policy Publications, Peterborough.

Cromie, S., Stephenson, B. and Monteith, D. (1995), The management of family firms: An empirical investigation, International Small Business, Vol.13, No.4, pp.11-34.

Daily, C. M. and Dollinger, M. J. (1992) An Empirical Examination of Ownership Structure in Family and Professionally Managed Firms, Family Business Review, Vol.5, No.2, pp.117-136.

Danco, L. (1975), Beyond Survival: A Guide for the Business Owner and His Family, The University Press, Cleveland.

Davis, J. (1982), The influence of life stage on father-son work relationships in family companies, Doctoral dissertation, Harvard University, Massachusetts.

Davis, J. (2006), Governance of the Family Business, Harvard Business School Cases, Massachusetts.

Davis, W., Dibrell, C., Craig, J. and Green, J. (2013), The Effects of Goal Orientation and Client Feedback on the Adaptive Behaviors of Family Enterprise Advisors, Family Business Review, Vol.26, No.3, pp.215-234.

Dawson, A. and Mussolino, D. (2014), Exploring what makes family firms different: Discrete or overlapping constructs in the literature?, Family Business Strategy, Vol.5, No.2, pp.169-183.

De Wit, B. and Meyer, R. (2010), Strategy Process, Content, Context: An international perspective, Cengage Learning, Hampshire.

Dion, K.L. (2000), Group cohesion: From" field of forces" to multidimensional construct, Group Dynamics: Theory, Research, and Practice, Vol.4, No.1, pp.7-26.

Donckels, R. and Fröhlich, E. (1991) Are Family Businesses Really Different? European Experiences from STRATOS, Family Business Review, Vol.4, No.2, pp.149-160.

European Union (2015), User guide to the SME Definition, Publications Office of the European Union, Luxembourg.

Fama, E.F. and Jensen, M.C. (1983), Separation of Ownership and Control, Law and Economics, Vol.26, No.2, pp.301-325.

Family Business Institute (2017a), Succession Planning. Available at: https://www.familybusinessinstitute.com/consulting/succession-planning/

Family Business Institute (2017b), Family Governance. Available at: https://www.familybusinessinstitute.com/consulting/family-governance/

Family Firm Institute (2017), Global Data Points. Available at: http://www.ffi.org/page/globaldatapoints

Filatotchev, I., Lien, Y. and Piesse, J. (2005), Corporate Governance and Performance in Publicly Listed, Family-Controlled Firms: Evidence from Taiwan, Asia Pacific Journal of Management, Vol.22, No.3, pp.257-283.

Filatotchev, I. (2007), Corporate Governance and the Firm's Dynamics: Contingencies and Complementarities, Management Studies, Vol.44, No.6, pp.1041-1056.

Forbes, D.P. and Milliken, F.J. (1999), Cognition and Corporate Governance: Understanding Boards of Directors as Strategic Decision-Making Groups, Academy of Management Review, Vol.24, No.3, pp.489-506.

Frishkoff, P. and Frishkoff, P. (2008), Leadership in Family Enterprise event (An inspiration for Sharma, P. et al, 2013). Available at: http://www.patandpaul.com/

Gabrielsson, J. (2007), Boards of directors in small and medium-sized industrial firms: Examining the effects of the board's working style on board task performance, International Small Business Journal, Vol.25, No.5, pp.511-537.

Gabrielsson, J. and Winlund, H. (2000), Boards of Directors in Small and Medium-Sized Industrial Firms: Examining the Effects of the Board's Working Style on Board Task Performance, Entrepreneurship and Regional Development, Vol.12, No.4, pp.311-330.

Gallo, M.A. (1995), The Role of Family Business and Its Distinctive Characteristic Behavior in Industrial Activity, Family Business Review, Vol.8, No.2, pp.83-97.

Garratt, B. (2010), The Fish Rots From The Head: The Crisis in our Boardrooms: Developing the Crucial Skills of the Competent Director, Profile Books, London.

Gersick, K., Davis, J, McCollom-Hampton, M. and Lansberg, I. (1996), Generation to Generation: Life Cycles of the Family Business, Harvard Business School Press, Massachusetts.

Gimeno, A., Baulenas, G. and Coma-Gros, J. (2010), Family Business Models: Practical Solutions for the Family Business, Palgrave Macmillan, Basingstoke.

Gleason, P. (2004), Effective entrepreneurial company boards, Independent Director Quarterly Review, Summer, pp.1-5.

Gomez-Mejia, L.R., Tosi, H. and Hinkin, T. (1987), Managerial control, performance, and executive compensation, Academy of Management, Vol.30, No.1, pp.51-70.

Gregory, H. and R.T. Simmelkjaer (2002), Comparative Study of Corporate Governance Codes Relevant to the European Union and its Members States on Behalf of the European Commission, Weil, Gotshal, and Manges, LLP, New York.

Gudmundson, D., Hartman, A.E. and Tower, B.C. (1999), Strategic Orientation: Differences between Family and Nonfamily Firms, Family Business Review, Vol.12, No.1, pp.27-39.

Haag, K. (2012), Rethinking family business succession: from a problem to solve to an ongoing practice, Doctoral thesis, Jönköping International Business School, Sweden.

Habbershon, T.G. and Williams, M.L. (1999), A Resource-Based Framework for Assessing the Strategic Advantages of Family Firms, Family Business Review, Vol.12, No.1, pp.1-25.

He, J. and Huang, Z. (2011). Board informal hierarchy and firm financial performance: Exploring a tacit structure guiding boardroom interactions, Academy of Management, Vol.54, No.6, pp.1119-1139.

Handler, W.C. (1990), Succession in Family Firms: A Mutual Role Adjustment between Entrepreneur and Next-generation Family Members, Entrepreneurship Theory and Practice, Vol.15, No.1, pp.37-51.

Hendry, J. (2002), The Principal's Other Problems: Honest Incompetence and the Specification of Objectives, Academy of Management Review, Vol.27, No.1, pp.98-113.

Hendry, K. and Kiel, G.C. (2004), The Role of the Board in Firm Strategy: integrating agency and organisational control perspectives,

Corporate Governance: An International Review, Vol.12, No.4, pp.500-520.

Higgs, D. (2002), Review of the role and effectiveness of non-executive directors, Department of Trade and Industry, UK Government, London.

Hira, N.A. (2007), You raised them, now manage them, Fortune, May 28, pp. 38-47.

Howe, N. and Strauss, W. (2000), Millennials Rising: The Next Great Generation, Vintage Books, New York.

Hoy, F. and Sharma, P. (2010), Entrepreneurial Family Firms, Pearson, New York.

Huse, M. (2000), Boards of directors in SMEs: A review and research agenda, Entrepreneurship and Regional Development, Vol.12, No.4, pp.271-290.

IFB (2017), Family Business Challenges, Institute for Family Business.

Available at: http://www.ifb.org.uk/learn/family-business-challenges/

IFB (2008), The UK Family Business Sector: An Institute for Family Business report by Capital Economics, Edward Elgar Publishing, Cheltenham.

IOD (2011), Corporate Governance Guidance and Principles for Unlisted Companies in Europe, Institute of Directors (2016), London. Available at: https://www.iod.com/Portals/0/PDFs/Campaigns%20and%20Reports/Corporate%20Governance/Governance%20code%20for%20unlisted%20companies.pdf?ver=2016-11-29-134715-607

International Council for Small Business (2017), UN Adopts Resolution Designating Micro-, Small and Medium-sized Enterprises International Day, April 6. Available at: https://www.icsb.org/un-adopts-resolution-designating-micro-small-medium-sized-enterprises-international-day/

Jaskiewicz, P. and Klein, S. (2007). The impact of goal alignment on board composition and board size in family businesses, Business Research, Vol.60, No.10, pp.1080-1089.

Jiang, Y. and Peng, M.W. (2010), Principal-principal conflicts during crisis. Asia Pacific Journal of Management, Vol.28, No.4, pp.683-695.

Johannisson B. and Huse M. (2000), Recruiting outside board members in the small family business: An ideological challenge, Entrepreneurship and Regional Development, Vol.12, No.4, pp.353-378.

Johnson, G., Whittington, R. and Scholes, K. (2011), Exploring Strategy: Text & Cases, Pearson Education, Harlow.

Jorissen, A., Laveren, E., Martens, R., and Reheul, A.-M. (2005). Real versus sample-based differences in comparative family business research. Family Business Review, Vol.18, No.3, pp.229-246.

Judge, W.Q. Jr. (1989). Toward a Theory of Board Involvement in the Strategic Decision Process, Doctoral dissertation, The University of North Carolina, Chapter Hill.

Kang, H., Cheng, M. and Gray, S.J. (2007). Corporate governance and board composition: Diversity and independence of Australian boards. Corporate Governance: An International Review, Vol.15, No.2, pp.194-207.

Kaye, K. (2005), The Dynamics of Family Business: Building Trust and Resolving Conflict, iUniverse, New York.

Kenyon-Rouvinez, D. and Ward, J. (2005), Family Business Key Issues, Palgrave Macmillan, London.

Knell, A. (2006), Corporate Governance: How to Add Value to your Company, Elsevier, London.

Lansberg, I. (1999), Succeeding Generations: Realizing the Dream of Families in Business, Harvard Business School Press, Massachusetts.

Leach, P. (1994), The Stoy Hayward guide to the family business, Kogan Page, London.

Leach, P. (2011), Family Businesses: The Essentials, Profile Books, London, UK.

Litz, R. (2008), Two sides of a one-sided phenomenon: Conceptualizing the family business and business family as a Möbius strip, Family Business Review, Vol.21, No.3, pp.217-236.

Long, T. (2007), The evolution of FTSE 250 boards of directors: Key factors influencing board performance and effectiveness, General Management, Vol.32, No.3, pp.45-60.

Lyman, A.R. (1991), Customer service: Does family ownership make a difference?. Family Business Review, Vol.4, No.3, pp.303-324.

Mallin, C. and Ow-Yong, K. (1998), Corporate governance in small companies; the alternative investment market, Corporate Governance: An International Review, Vol.6, No.4, pp.224-232.

Martin, C. (2005), From high maintenance to high productivity; what managers need to know about Generation Y, Industrial and Commercial Training, Vol.37, No.1, pp.39-44.

Miller, D., Le Breton-Miller, I., Lester, R. and Canella, A. (2007), Are Family Firms Really Superior Performers, Corporate Finance, Vol.13, No.5, pp.829-858.

McGivern, C. (1989), The dynamics of management succession: A model of chief executive succession in the small family firm, Family Business Review, Vol.2, No.4, pp.401-411.

Merson, R. (2004), Owners, Profile Books, London.

Miller, D. and Le Bretton-Miller, I. (2005), Managing for the long run: Lessons in competitive advantage from great family businesses, Harvard Business School Press, Massachusetts.

Monks, R.A. and Minow, N. (2008), Corporate Governance, Blackwell Business, Cambridge.

OECD (1997), Small Businesses, Job Creation and Growth: Facts, Obstacles and Best Practices. Available at: https://www.oecd.org/cfe/smes/2090740.pdf

OECD (2017), G20/OECD Principles of Corporate Governance. Available at: https://www.oecd.org/daf/ca/Corporate-Governance-Principles-ENG.pdf

O'Leary, S. (2012), Impact of entrepreneurship teaching in higher education on the employability of scientists and engineers, Industry and Higher Education Journal, Vol.26, No.6, pp.431-442.

O'Leary, S. (2013), Collaborations in higher education with employers and their influence on graduate employability; an institutional project, Higher Education Academy Journal Enhancing Learning in the Social Sciences, Vol.5, No.1, pp.37-50.

O'Leary, S. and Swaffin-Smith (2013), An appraisal of family enterprise advisors as enhancers of both group performance and individual family member employability profiles, Regent's Working Papers in Business & Management, RWPBM1307.

O'Leary, S. and Swaffin-Smith, C. (2016), Organic model to reflect the transitional nature of family firms, The Marketing Review, Vol.16, No.3, pp.285-297.

Olson, P.D., Zuiker, V.S., Danes, S.M., Stafford, K., Heck, R.K.Z. and Duncan, K.A. (2003), Impact of family and business on family business sustainability, Business Venturing, Vol.18, No.5, pp.639-666.

O'Reilly, B. (2000), Meet the future, Fortune, July, pp.144-168.

Onuoha, B.C. (2012), Professionalizing Family Businesses in the South-East Region of Nigeria, International Business and Management, Vol.5, No.1, pp.153-161.

Oxford English Dictionary (2014), Oxford University Press, Oxford.

Poutziouris, P.Z (2006), The structure and performance of the UK family business PLC economy, in Poutziouris, P.Z., Smyrnios K.X. and Klein S.B. (Eds.), Handbook of Research on Family Businesses. Edward Elgar, Cheltenham.

Poutziouris, P.Z and Chittenden, C. (1996), Family business or business families?, The Institute of Small Business Affairs Research Series, Monograph 2.

Pieper, T. and Klein, S. (2007), The bulleye: A systems approach to modeling family firms, Family Business Review, Vol.20, No.4, pp.301-319.

Poza, E. (2010), Family Business, South-Western Cengage Learning, Mason Ohio.

Reay, T. (2009), Family-business meta-identity, institutional pressures, and ability to respond to entrepreneurial opportunities, Entrepreneurship Theory and Practice, Vol.33, No.6, pp.1265-1270.

Reay, T., Pearson, A. and Gibb-Dyer (2013), Advising family enterprise: Examining the role of family firm advisors, Family Business Review, Vol.26, No.3, pp.209-214.

Rothwell, W.J. (2010), Effective succession planning: Ensuring leadership continuity and building talent from within, AMACOM Division of American Management Association.

Rutherford, M., Muse, L. and Oswald, S. (2006), A new perspective on the developmental model for family business, Family Business Review, Vol.19, No.4, pp.317-333.

Schulze, W.S., Lubatkin, M.H., Dino, R.N. and Buchholtz, A.K. (2001), Agency Relationships in Family Firms: Theory and Evidence, Organization Science, Vol.12, No.2, pp.99-116.

Searle, R.H. (2010), Recruitment and Selection, in Wood, G. and Collins, D.C. (Eds.), Human Resources Management: A critical introduction, Palgrave MacMillan, London.

Shanker, M.C. and Astrachan, J.H. (1996), Myths and Realities: Family Businesses' Contribution to the Us Economy; a Framework for Assessing Family Business Statistics, Family Business Review, Vol.9, No.2, pp.107-119.

Sharma, P. (2004), An overview of the field of family business studies: Current status and directions for future, Family Business Review, Vol.19, No.1, pp.1-36.

Sharma, P., Chrisman, J.J. and Chua, J.H. (1997), Strategic management of the family business: Past research and future challenges. Family business review, Vol.10, No.1, pp.1-35.

Sharma, P., Blunden, R., Labaki, R., Michael-Tsabari, N. and Algarin, J. (2013), Analyzing family business cases: Tools and techniques, Case Research Journal, Vol.33, No.2. pp.1-20.

Sharma, P., Chrisman, J.J. and Chua, J.H. (1996), A review and annotated bibliography of family business studies, Kluwer Academic Publishers, Massachusetts.

Sharma, P. & Irving, P.G. (2005), Four bases of family business successor commitment: Antecedents and consequences, Entrepreneurship Theory and Practice, Vol.29, No.1, pp.13-33.

Singer, J. and Donoho, C. (1992), Strategic management planning for the successful family business, Business and Entrepreneurship, Vol.4, No.3, pp.39-51.

Smith, B. and Amoako-Adu, B. (1999), Management succession and financial performance of family controlled firms, Corporate Finance, Vol. 5, No.4, pp.341–368.

Sonnenfeld, J.A. and Spence, P.L (1989), The Parting Patriarch of a Family Firm, Family Business Review, Vol.2, No.4, pp.355-375.

Sorenson, R. (2011), Family Business and Social Capital, Edward Elgar, Cheltenham.

Stafford, K., Duncan, K.A., Dane, S. and Winter, M. (1999), A Research Model of Sustainable Family Businesses, Family Business Review, Vol.12, No.3, pp.197-208.

Steier, L.P. and Miller, D. (2010), Pre- and post-succession governance philosophies in entrepreneurial family firms, Family Business Strategy, Vol.1, No.3, pp.145-154.

Strike, V. (2013), The most trusted advisor and the subtle advice process in family firms, Family Business Review, Vol.26, No.3, pp.293-313.

Su, E. and Dou, J. (2013), How does knowledge sharing among advisors from different disciplines affect the quality of the services provided to the family business client? An investigation from the family business advisor's perspective, Family Business Review, Vol.26, No.3, pp.256-270.

Sundaramurthy, C., and Lewis, M. (2003), Control and collaboration: Paradoxes of governance. Academy of Management Review, Vol.28, No.3, pp.397-415.

Swaffin-Smith, C., Woolliams, P. and Tomeko, J. (2000), Towards a Unified Model for Small to Medium Enterprise Business Paradigms, Earlybrave Publications, Brentwood.

Tagiuri R. and Davis J. (1982), Bivalent Attributes of The Family Firm, Division of Research, Harvard Business School. Reprint at Davis, J.A. and Tagiuri, R. (1996).

Tagiuri, R., and Davis, J.A. (1992), On the goals of successful family companies, Family Business Review, Vol.5, No.1, pp.43-62.

Tagiuri, R., and Davis, J. (1996), Bivalent attributes of the family firm, Family business review, Vol.9, No.2, pp.199-208.

Terjesen, S., Vinnicombe, S. and Freeman, C. (2007), Attracting generation Y graduates, Career Development International, Vol.12, No.6, pp.504-522.

Tricker, R.I. (2009), The independent director: A study of the non-executive director and of the audit committee, Tolley, Croydon.

United Nations (2017), Micro-, Small and Medium-sized Enterprises Day, Resolution A/RES/71/279 adopted by the General Assembly on 6 April. Available at: www.un.org/en/ga/search/view_doc.asp?symbol=A/RES/71/279

Wageman, R. (1995), Interdependence and group effectiveness, Administrative Science Quarterly, pp.145-180.

Walker, E. and Brown, A. (2004), What success factors are important to small business owners? International Small Business, Vol.22, No.6, pp.577-594.

Ward, J. (1987), Keeping the family business healthy: How to plan for continuing growth, profitability, and family leadership, Jossey-Bass, San Francisco.

Ward, J. (1992), Creating Effective Boards for Private Enterprises, Jossey-Bass, San Francisco.

Ward, J. (2004), Perpetuating the Family Business, Palgrave Macmillan, Basingstoke.

Ward, J.L. and Aronoff, C.E. (2011), Family Business Governance: Maximizing Family and Business Potential, Palgrave Macmillan, Basingstoke.

Westhead P. (1997), Ambitions, 'external' environment and strategic factor differences between family and non-family companies, Entrepreneurship and Regional Development, Vol.9, No.2, pp.127-157.

Whisler, T.L. (1988), The Role of the Board in the Threshold Firm, Family Business Review, Vol.1, No.3, pp.309-312.

Zahra, S.A., Filatotchev, I. and Wright, M. (2009), How do threshold firms sustain corporate entrepreneurship? The role of boards and absorptive capacity, Business Venturing, Vol.24, No.3, pp.248-260.

Zingales, L. (1997), Corporate Governance, in Palgrave Dictionary of Economics and Law, Oxford University Press, Oxford.

www.ingramcontent.com/pod-product-compliance
Lightning Source LLC
Chambersburg PA
CBHW041311210326
41599CB00003B/69